DEPARTMENTAL COACHING STOCK

The complete guide to all current
British Railways
Departmental Coaching Stock Vehicles

Roger Butcher
&
Peter Fox

Published by Platform 5 Publishing Ltd., Provincial House, Solly Street, Sheffield S1 4BA.

Printed by Bayliss Printing Co. Ltd., Turner Road, Worksop, Notts.

ISBN 0 906579 47 3

CONTENTS

INTRODUCTION

Since the first edition of 'Departmental Coaching Stock' was published in May 1984 there have not only been many additions and disposals of stock, but also a significant number of changes either in the base or the use of vehicles. This second edition has therefore been prepared to reflect the very latest situation.

Also presented for the very first time is a complete list of all coaching stock vehicles now in the internal user fleet.

The first point to be made is that all coaching stock converted for departmental use is numbered in the BR wagon number series. Essentially there are four regional series (DE, DM, DS, DW) and one all-region series (DB). This latter number series is the one to which all current conversions are placed. The numbering of internal user vehicles is a regional responsibility each region having its own range of numbers. Further notes on each number series will be found at the beginning of the relevant section.

Railways have always needed vehicles of both passenger and freight stock for their own internal purposes, i.e. non-revenue-earning vehicles. Such vehicles are known as service stock or more often departmental stock. The word "departmental" is derived because all non-revenue-earning vehicles are owned by one of the departments which have a specific responsibility for the operation or maintenance of the railway system.

The following departmental vehicles are included:

1. Former coaching stock types, including horse boxes, fish and fruit vans.
2. Non coaching stock types that have been converted or constructed primarily for use with coaching stock e.g. steam heating boiler vans.
3. Non coaching stock types that have been allocated numbers in the various departmental coaching stock series e.g. snowploughs.

Vehicles destined for scrap merchants or preservation societies are also included if still on the BR network.

The format of this second edition is current number, Carkind (Tops Code), location/allocation, current use, conversion date where known, followed by the build details of the original vehicle.

With the implementation of TOPS in 1973 each departmental vehicle acquired a prefix to indicate the department which owned it.

No prefix indicates it is a Regional Civil Engineer vehicle.

A Regional Mechanical and Electrical Engineer
C BREL
K Regional Signal and Telecommunications Engineer
L RM & EE Electrical Construction
R Research Department
T Traffic Department
X Stores Department
Z Public Relations and Publicity

The reorganization of BR's management structure in 1984 resulted in a reduction in the status of the various Heads of Departments on each region who are no longer referred to as "Chief". The conventional descriptions of CCE and CM & EE are thus replaced by RCE and RM & EE. However it will no doubt be a considerable time before this change is fully reflected on the brandings carried by departmental stock. 1984 saw the abolition of divisions, although in the case of civil engineering divisions, they are retained but are to be referred to in future as areas. This edition continues to use the term division.

CARKIND code comprises a three character code, usually painted adjacent to the vehicle number and indicates vehicle use. It is worth stating that Q indicates a former stock type departmental vehicle, whilst Z is a 2 axle or miscellaneous vehicle. Some ex-parcels stock are branded Z - even when the vehicle is recognised as formerly being coaching stock.

The second character indicates current use:

QP Staff, Dormitory
QQ Tool Van
QR Stores, Materials
QS Miscellaneous Operating Vehicle - Runner, Steam Heating Boiler Van, Loading Ramp.
QT Brake Van
QV General Equipment Carrier
QW Self Propelled Unit, Saloon
QX Specialist Equipment Vehicle - Instruction, Inspection, Mobile Office, Test Coach etc.
QY Electrification Equipment Vehicle.

Finally the third character indicates the power brake fitted, the codes being:

A Air brake
B Air brake, through vacuum pipe
O No power brake
Q No power brake, through air pipe
V Vacuum brake
W Vacuum brake, through air pipe
X Dual brake (air & vacuum)

It must be noted that CARKINDS listed herein may differ from official records or vehicle branding, but are correct for vehicle use, ie BTU Rerailing Equipment Vehicles are branded QV, but this publication records such vehicles as Tool Vans, QQ, since in effect they are one and the same.

As regards location/allocation the 'Lineside' formula is used. This indicates that:

(1) the location listed is the base from which the vehicle works and where it will most often be found.
(2) Where, after the base, the region of the vehicle is given, the vehicle may spend significant periods away from its base;
(3) Where the base is in brackets, this indicates that at the time of publication the vehicle had been at that location for a significant period, but in no way could it be considered a permanent base; and
(4) Where only the region and no specific location is stated, the vehicle is regularly on the move, often on a weekly basis, and to detail where it had last been seen would be misleading.

As regards current use, although there are often wide variations in the brands carried on vehicles with exactly the same usage, this publication has detailed each vehicle's use in a uniform way.

It should be noted that prior to June 1956, the two classes of accommodation generally available on Britain's Railways were known as "first and third" and as such build details refer to vehicle designation as built. Boat trains on the Southern Region, however, consisted of first, second and third class accommodation, until third class accommodation was abolished in Europe. The British third class was then renamed "second class". Certain LNER vehicles used on Great Eastern Section boat trains were also "second class".

Finally I would like to record my thanks to all those departmental enthusiasts who have for many years been regularly assisting me in my efforts to maintain an accurate and comprehensive register of BR departmental coaching stock. Their assistance in monitoring what happens in their own areas is particularly vital, as for BR to attempt to produce information in a suitable form for enthusiasts would be a very costly exercise for which there is no financial justification. Inevitably there are too many to individually mention, but particular thanks to Keith, Paul, Peter and Rowland.

Roger Butcher
April 1985

ABBREVIATIONS USED

1. Railway Companies and Regions etc.

BR	British Railways	LNER	London and North Eastern Railway
BREL	British Rail Engineering Ltd.	LNWR	London and North Western Railway
CR	Caledonian Railway	LSWR	London and South Western Railway
ECJS	East Coast Joint Stock	MR	Midland Railway
ER	Eastern Region of BR	NER	North Eastern Railway
GER	Great Eastern Railway	ScR	Scottish Region of BR.
GNR	Great Northern Railway	S&DJR	Somerset and Dorset Joint Railway
GWR	Great Western Railway	SECR	South Eastern and Chatham Railway
IoW	Isle of Wight	SR	Southern Railway or Southern Region of BR.
LMR	London Midland Region of BR		
LMS	London Midland and Scottish Railway	WR	Western Region of BR.

2. Coaching Stock Types

These consist generally of a one, two or three letter code, F for first class, S for second, T for third, C for composite (first & second or first & third). One letter only indicates a non-gangwayed vehicle. F, S, T or C followed by K indicates a gangwayed side corridor vehicle with lavatory, whereas gangwayed open coaches are followed with O. Semi-open vehicles are denoted as so. Non-gangwayed vehicles with lavatories are denoted by L. Open third (or second) class vehicles are denoted by the codes TTO (or TSO) by the LNER and BR if they have 2+2 seating, whereas 2+1 seating vehicles were known as TO or SO. The LMS, however referred to 2+2 seating vehicles as TO and 2+1 seating vehicles as RTO (R for refreshment, i.e. they were designed for use as third class diners). A "B" prefix indicates a brake vehicle. Similarly on BR, open dining cars without kitchens were classified as RFO, RSO and RUO (U = Unclassified seating). Catering vehicles with kitchens or bars are denoted as follows:

RB	Kitchen Buffet with Seating
RBK	BR Kitchen Buffet converted from RF
RC	Composite Restaurant car
RF	First Class Restaurant car
RK	Kitchen Car (no seats)
RKB	Kitchen - Buffet (no seats)
RMB	Miniature Buffet car
RU	Unclassified Restaurant car.

Sleeping cars are:

SLF	First Class Sleeping Car
SLSTP	Second Class Sleeping Car (Twin Berth with Pantry)
SLT	Third Class Sleeping Car
SLT(T)	Third Class Sleeping Car (Twin Berth)

The various van abbreviations are as follows:

B	Full Brake, bogie vehicle
BG	Full Brake, bogie vehicle, gangwayed
BY	Full Brake, four-wheeled
CCT	Covered Carriage Truck, four-wheeled
GUV	General Utility Van, bogie vehicle
HB	Horse box
PMV	Parcels and Miscellaneous Van

It should be noted that these above standard BR abbreviations and names for vans are used, even though the pre-nationalisation companies may have used other names. The exception is ex GWR and GWR-design vans where the code names are in common use today, e.g. Siphon G - Ventilated Milk Van (bogie) - used for general parcels traffic.

3. General Codes

APT Advanced Passenger Train
BRCW Birmingham Railway Carriage & Wagon Ltd.
BRUTE British Rail Universal Trolley Equipment
BSC British Steel Corporation
BTU Breakdown Train Unit
C&W Carriage & Wagon
CWR Continuous Welded Rail
DMU Diesel Multiple Unit
EML Euston—Manchester—Liverpool Electrification Scheme
EMU Electric Multiple Unit
GSU Glasgow Suburban Electrification Scheme
HST High Speed Train
IU Internal User
M & EE Mechanical & Electrical Engineer (applies to BR Headquarters)
MOD Ministry of Defence
NCL National Carriers Ltd.
ODM Outdoor Machinery
OHLM Overhead Line Maintenance
OOU Out of use
PAD Pre-Assembly Depot
POP Prototype APT Space Frame Vehicles
PSS Power Supply Section
RCE Regional Civil Engineer
RM & EE Regional Mechanical & Electrical Engineer (applies to Regions)
RTC Railway Technical Centre, followed by location
S&T Signal & Telecommunications
TMD Traction Maintenance Depot
TOPS Total Operations Processing System
* Departmental number not carried
‡ Full details not available for this vehicle
U/F Underframe

ADB975091 'Mentor' (Test Car 3) parked at the Railway Technical Centre, Derby on 26th July 1982. [C. J. Tuffs

REFERENCES

The following references on departmental stock are available:

(1) Departmental Coaching Stock. DB97xxxx Series. £0.90.

(2) Departmental Coaching Stock. Southern Region. Out of Print

(3) Departmental Coaching Stock. Western Region. £0.90.

The above three books were published by Lineside and give comprehensive and accurate information on those vehicles no longer in current BR stock and therefore not included in this publication. Details are given of vehicles scrapped including where, when and by whom, vehicles surviving as grounded bodies either on BR or on private land, vehicles sold for preservation, camping coaches, vehicles sold for further use, i.e. to Associated British Ports.

(4) Track Machines. Roger Butcher. Platform 5. £2.50.

The following references on coaching stock are available:

(5) Locomotive Hauled Mark 1 Coaching Stock of British Railways. Keith Parkin. Published by Historical Model Railway Society (HMRS). £10.95 (limp cover). Note: Hardback version out of print.

(6) Gresley's Coaches. Michael Harris. Pub.: David & Charles, 1973.

(7) Great Western Coaches: From 1890, Michael Harris. Pub.: David & Charles 1984 (revised edition).

(8) An Illustrated History of LMS Coaches. R.J. Essery & David Jenkinson. OPC. (Out of print).

(9) An Illustrated History of LNWR Coaches. David Jenkinson. OPC. 1978.

(10) A Register of West Coast Joint Stock. R.M. Casserley & P.A. Millard. HMRS 1980. £8.40.

(11) A Pictorial Record of Great Western Coaches Parts 1 & 2. J.H. Russell. OPC.

(12) Maunsell's S.R. Steam Passenger Stock 1923-1939. David Gould. Oakwood Press 1978. £4.20.

(13) Bullied's S.R. Steam Passenger Stock. David Gould. Oakwood Press 1980. £3.00.

(14) Carriage Stock of the S.E. & C.R. David Gould. Oakwood Press 1976. £3.50.

(15) Carriage Stock of the L.B. & S.C.R. P.J. Newbury. Oakwood Press 1976. Out of Print.

(16) Service Stock of the Southern Railway. R.W. Kidner. Oakwood Press 1980. £2.70.

(17) A Register of G.W.R. Absorbed Coaching Stock 1922/3. E.R. Mountford. Oakwood Press. £4.50.

(18) Carriage Stock of Minor Standard Gauge Railways. R.W. Kidner. Oakwood Press. £2.70.

(19) Midland Carriages - An Illustrated Review. David Jenkinson and Bob Essery. OPC 1984. £13.95.

(20) Midland Railway Carriages Vol. 1. R. E. Lacy & George Dow. Wild Swan 1984. £12.50.

References 1, 3 and 4 on departmental stock and references 5, 9 to 20 on coaching stock are available from our Mail Order Department. Please enclose contribution to postage and packing: 20p for one item, 10p for each subsequent item. Orders over £12 post free. Address: Mail Order Dept., Platform 5 Publishing Ltd., 15 Abbeydale Park Rise, Sheffield, S17 3PB.

DB NUMBER SERIES

Most DB-series vehicles are former BR designed coaches. It should be noted that the diagram numbers quoted are the original BR diagram numbers, not the present ones as used in "Coaching Stock Pocket Book", the reason being that many of the vehicle types converted did not survive long enough for diagram numbers according to the new scheme to be allotted. BR Wagon lot numbers and dates of conversion are quoted where applicable.

The DB97xxxx series was first used at the end of 1966, the intention being that all service vehicles converted from condemned coaching stock could be numbered in one series. However until 1970 this number series was little used as almost all service vehicles continued to be numbered into the various regional series. From 1970 the DB975xxx series began in earnest, although until 1979 some of the regional number series were used. Also in 1970 DB975500-37 were allocated, and so when towards the end of 1975 ABD975481-99 were allocated, the series jumped to DB975538. By the end of 1980 the DB975xxx series had been completed and as the DB976xxx series was in use for service vehicles converted from condemned freight stock, the series jumped to DB977000 and at the time of writing the highest number allocated is ADB977292.

A comprehensive history of all DB97xxxx vehicles is available from our mail order department. (See section on references). News on additions to the DB97xxxx fleet and disposals of all the departmental fleets will be regularly found in the special monthly feature on departmentals in Rail Enthusiast.

Purpose-built (as opposed to conversions) DB coaches are numbered in a separate series (p.35).

DB963904	QSW	Glasgow North Division. Runner for Crane DRT81305. Converted on lot 3598, 1966 as Freightliner Brake Van. *Formerly BR Mk1 BT S43383, to dia 372 on lot 30151 Swindon 1955.*
DB963925	QSW	Glasgow South Division. Runner for Crane DRT81304. Converted on lot 3643, 1967 as Freightliner Brake Van. *Formerly BR Mk1 BT E43115, to dia 371 on lot 30045 York 1955.*
DB963947	QSW	Newport Division. Runner for Crane DRT81317. Converted on lot 3643, 1967 as Freightliner Brake Van. *Formerly BR Mk1 BT SC43314, to dia 371 on lot 30087 York 1955.*
ADB963952	QQV	MR. BTU Tool Van. Converted on lot 3643, 1967 as Freightliner Brake Van. *Formerly BR Mk1 BT SC43326, to dia 371 on lot 30087 York 1955.*
ADB963953	QQV	IM. BTU Tool Van. Converted on lot 3643, 1967 as Freightliner Brake Van. *Formerly BR Mk1 BT SC43341, to dia 371 on lot 30087 York 1955.*
RDB975000	QXA	RTC, Derby. Laboratory Coach 1. Converted on lot 3733, 1970. *Formerly BR Mk1 RSO M1003, to dia 56 on lot 30014 York 1951.*
RDB975002	QXA	RTC, Derby. Laboratory Coach 3. Converted on lot 3733, 1970. *Formerly BR Mk1 RSO M1005, to dia 56 on lot 30014 York 1951.*
RDB975003	QWV	RTC, Mickleover. Laboratory 16 'Gemini'. *Formerly DMBS (Battery powered) SC79998, to dia 406 on lot 30368.*
RDB975004	QWV	RTC, Mickleover. Laboratory 16 'Gemini'. *Formerly DMCL (Battery powered) SC79999, to dia 442 on lot 30369.*
DB975007	QWV	OC. Ultrasonic Test Train. Converted on lot 3732, 1970. *Formerly Derby Lightweight DMDS M79018, to dia 503 on lot 30123.*
DB975008	QWV	OC. Ultrasonic Test Train. Converted on lot 3732, 1970. *Formerly Derby Lightweight DTCL M79612, to dia 509 on lot 30124.*
ADB975009	QQV	MR. BTU Tool Van. *Formerly BR Mk1 BT E43125, to dia 371 on lot 30045 York 1955*
RDB975010	QWV	RTC, Derby. Test Coach 'Iris', Radio Tests. *Formerly Derby Lightweight single unit DMBS M79900, to dia 514 on lot 30380.*
DB975017	QPV	WR. RCE Staff & Dormitory Coach for Ballast Cleaner DR76322. Converted on lot 3738, 1970 as Welding Instruction Coach. *Formerly BR Mk1 BTO W9207, to dia 183 on lot 30170 Doncaster 1955*
TDB975023	QWV	RG. Route Learning Car. *Formerly Class 122 DMBS W55001, to dia 539 on lot 30419 Gloucester 1958. Carried DB975073 in error.*
ADB975024	QPV	CF. BTU Staff & Dormitory Coach. *Formerly BR Mk1 BCK W21070, to dia 172 on lot 30133 Metro-Cammell 1955*

TDB975025 QWA SL. SR General Managers' Saloon. Converted on lot 3746, 1970.
Formerly Class 201 TSRB S60755, to dia 678 on lot 30393, 1958.

ADB975027 EZ5X Strawberry Hill EMU Depot. RM & EE Test Coach, Rolling Stock Development Trials, Converted 1969.
Formerly Class 501 DMBS M61162, to dia 403 on lot 30326 Eastleigh 1957.

ADB975032 EZ5 Strawberry Hill EMU Depot. RM & EE Test Coach 'Mars'. Converted 1969.
Formerly Class 501 DTS M75165, to dia on lot 30328 Eastleigh 1957.

ADB975033 QPV LA. BTU Staff & Tool Coach.
Formerly BR Mk1 BTO W9214, to dia 183 on lot 30170 Doncaster 1955

RDB975036 QXV RTC, Derby. Laboratory Coach 22, Tribometer Stores.
Formerly BR Mk1 BTO M9234, to dia 183 on lot 30170 Doncaster 1955

ADB975038 QRV ZL. Stores Coach, formerly 'ENPARTS'.
Formerly BR Mk1 BTO W9258, to dia 183 on lot 30170 Doncaster 1955

TDB975042 QWV LMR. Route Learning Car.
Formerly Class 122 DMBS M55019, to dia 539 on lot 30419 Gloucester 1958.

RDB975046 QXX RTC, Derby. Laboratory Coach 11.
Formerly BR Mk1 BTK S34249, to dia 181 on lot 30021 Eastleigh 1952

KDB975047 QPV Cocklebury Sidings, Swindon. S&T Contractor's Staff & Dormitory Coach.
Formerly BR Mk1 BTK W34769, to dia 182 on lot 30156 Wolverton 1955.

ADB975051 QXX CE. ZC Test Train Coach. Converted on lot 3786, 1972.
Formerly BR Mk1 BTK M34133, to dia 181 on lot 30025 Wolverton 1951.

ADB975054 QPV HT. BTU Staff Coach. Converted on lot 3734, 1970.
Formerly BR Mk1 BTO E9200, to dia 183 on lot 30170 Doncaster 1955.

ADB975055 QQV TE. BTU Tool Van. Converted on lot 3735, 1970.
Formerly LNER Thompson BG E70584E, to dia 327 built York 1945.

ZDB975056 QXV ZN. Generator Van. Converted on lot 3736, 1970.
Formerly BR Mk1 Horse Box M96300, to dia 751 on lot 30146 Earlstown 1957.

DB975057 QPV WR. RCE Staff & Dormitory Coach for Ballast Cleaner DR76210.
Formerly BR Mk1 BTK S34635, to dia 182 on lot 30143 Charles Roberts, 1954.

DB975058 QPV Ashton Gate Engineers' Yard, Bristol. RCE Staff & Dormitory Coach for Tunnel Inspection Train.
Formerly BR Mk1 BTK S34619, to dia 182 on lot 30142 Gloucester 1955.

The following vehicles are Electrification Section, BRB, staff coaches (QYV or QYW) and were converted on lot 3775, 1971 from BR MK1 TKS (975062-9) to dia 146 and BTKS (975071/2) to dia 181:

No.	*Location*	*Formerly*	*Build Details*		
LDB975062	(ZD for repair)	M24062	Lot 30002	Derby	1951
LDB975064	(ZD for repair)	M24067	Lot 30002	Derby	1951
LDB975065	(ZD for repair)	M24134	Lot 30002	Derby	1951
LDB975066	(York)	M24140	Lot 30002	Derby	1951
LDB975068	(Ipswich Engineers' Yard)	M24189	Lot 30015	Doncaster	1951
LDB975069	(Diss)	M24320	Lot 30020	Eastleigh	1952
LDB975071	Rugby Maintenance Depot	M34140	Lot 30025	Wolverton	1951
LDB975072	Wigan Bamfurlong Sidings OOU	M34695	Lot 30156	Wolverton	1955

ZDB975074 QXX Salisbury. Exhibition Coach. Converted on lot 3740, 1970.
Formerly BR Mk1 TK M24119, to dia 146 on lot 30002 Derby 1951.

RDB975076 QXX RTC, Derby. Tribometer Coach.
Formerly BR Mk1 BTK E34500, to dia 181 on lot 30060 Gloucester 1954.

ADB975077 QPV GM. BTU Staff Coach. Converted on lot 3743, 1970.
Formerly BR Mk1 BCK SC21018, to dia 171 on lot 30006 Metro-Cammell 1954.

ADB975078 QQV GD. BTU Tool Van. Converted on lot 3744, 1970.
Formerly BR Mk1 BTK E34828, to dia 182 on lot 30220 Gloucester 1955.

ADB975080 QQV TO. BTU Tool Van. Converted on lot 3747, 1970 to replace DE320294.
Formerly BR Mk1 TK M25079, to dia 147 on lot 30155 Wolverton 1956.

RDB975081 QXX RTC, Derby. Test Coach. Converted on lot 3748, 1970.
Formerly BR Mk1 BSK M35313, to dia 181 on lot 30699 Wolverton 1962.

ADB975082 QQV Basingstoke. BTU Tool Van. OOU. Converted on lot 3749, 1970.
Formerly BR Mk1 BTO W9261, to dia 183 on lot 30170 Doncaster 1955.

ADB975083 QPV LE. BTU Staff & Tool Coach. Converted on lot 3749, 1970 to replace DW150303.
Formerly BR Mk1 BTK W34632, to dia 182 on lot 30143 Charles Roberts 1954.

ADB975084 QPV LA. BTU Staff & Dormitory Coach. Converted on lot 3749, 1970 to replace DW150219.
Formerly BR Mk1 BTK W34756, to dia 182 on lot 30157 Wolverton 1955.

ADB975085 QPV RG. BTU Staff & Tool Coach. Converted on lot 3749, 1970.
Formerly BR Mk1 BTK S34622, to dia 182 on lot 30142 Gloucester 1955.

ADB975087 QQV NH. BTU Tool Van. Converted on lot 3750, 1970.
Formerly BR Mk1 BTK M34289, to dia 181 on lot 30032 Wolverton 1952.

ADB975088 QQV CH. BTU Tool Van. Converted on lot 3750, 1970.
Formerly BR Mk1 BTK M34132, to dia 181 on lot 30025 Wolverton 1951.

RDB975089 QWV RTC, Derby. Track Recording Car.
Formerly Class 103 DMBS M50396, to dia 635 on lot 30286 Park Royal 1957.

RDB975090 QWV RTC, Derby. Track Recording Car.
Formerly Class 103 DTCL M56162, to dia 645 on lot 30287 Park Royal 1957.

ADB975091 QXX RTC, Derby. M & EE Test Coach 'Mentor'. Converted on lot 3753, 1971.
Formerly BR Mk1 BTK W34615, to dia 182 on lot 30142 Gloucester 1955.

The following are S & T cable drum carriers (QVV) and were converted on lot 3761, 1971 from BR Mk1s:

No.	*Location*	*Formerly*	*Type*	*Dia.*	*Build Details*		
KDB975097	(Wigston)	M34617	BTK	182	Lot 30142	Gloucester	1955
KDB975098	(Preston Dock St)	M34709	BTK	181	Lot 30156	Wolverton	1955
KDB975099	(Chester C&W Shops)	M34127	BTK	181	Lot 30025	Wolverton	1951
KDB975100	(Preston Dock St)	M34710	BTK	181	Lot 30156	Wolverton	1955
KDB975101	(Chester C&W Shops)	M34691	BTK	181	Lot 30156	Wolverton	1955
KDB975102	(Wigston)	M34658	BTK	181	Lot 30156	Wolverton	1955
KDB975103	(Wigston)	M34705	BTK	181	Lot 30156	Wolverton	1955
KDB975104	(Wigston)	M15392	CK	126	Lot 30075	Derby	1954
KDB975105	(Wigston)	M15389	CK	126	Lot 30075	Derby	1954
KDB975106	(Wigston)	M24745	TK	146	Lot 30073	Wolverton	1953
KDB975107	(Wigston)	M15690	CK	126	Lot 30158	Wolverton	1956
KDB975108	(Wigston)	M34688	BTK	181	Lot 30156	Wolverton	1955
KDB975109	(Wigston)	M15341	CK	126	Lot 30033	Derby	1953
KDB975110	(Preston Dock St)	M15129	CK	126	Lot 30005	Metro-Cammell	1952
KDB975111	(Chester C&W Shops)	M34512	BTK	181	Lot 30061	Charles Roberts	1954
KDB975112	(Preston Dock St)	M34470	BTK	181	Lot 30060	Gloucester	1953
KDB975113	(Wigston)	M15454	CK	126	Lot 30062	Metro-Cammell	1954
KDB975114	(Chester C&W Shops)	M24420	TK	146	Lot 30030	Derby	1953

ADB975118 QPV FH. BTU Staff & Tool Coach.
Formerly BR Mk1 BTK M34265, to dia 181 on lot 30021 Eastleigh 1951.

ADB975123 QPV HM. BTU Staff Coach. Converted on lot 3769, 1971.
Formerly BR Mk1 BCK E21011, to dia 171 on lot 30006 Metro-Cammell 1954.

ADB975127 QPV FH. BTU Staff & Tool Coach. Converted on lot 3772, 1971 to replace DE320867.
Formerly BR Mk1 BTK E34754, to dia 182 on lot 30157 Wolverton 1955.

ADB975128 QPV CA. BTU Staff & Tool Coach. Converted on lot 3772, 1971 to replace DE320146.
Formerly BR Mk1 BTK E34414, to dia 181 on lot 30064 Wolverton 1953.

ADB975129 QQV NC. BTU Tool Van. Converted on lot 3773, 1971 to replace DE320668.
Formerly BR Mk1 BTK E34495, to dia 181 on lot 30064 Wolverton 1953.

ADB975132 QQX TO. BTU Tool Van. Converted on lot 3776, 1971.
Formerly BR Mk1 BTK M34074, to dia 181 on lot 30003 Derby 1951.

ADB975133 QQV AN. BTU Tool Van. Converted on lot 3776, 1971.
Formerly BR Mk1 BTK M34049, to dia 181 on lot 30003 Derby 1971.

ADB975134 QQV SP. BTU Tool Van. Converted on lot 3776, 1971.
Formerly BR Mk1 BTK M34071, to dia 181 on lot 30003 Derby 1951.

RDB975136 QXX RTC, Derby. Laboratory Coach 12. Converted on lot 3801, 1972 as Stores Coach for APT Vehicles.
Formerly BR Mk1 BTK M34505, to dia 181 on lot 30061 Charles Roberts 1954.

ADB975140	QPV	(New Cross Gate C&W Shops). PSS Staff & Tool Brake Van. Converted on lot 3779, 1971. *Formerly SR BY S436S, to dia 3092 on RSCO A928 Ashford/Eastleigh 1937.*
ADB975141	QPV	Horsham. PSS Staff & Tool Brake Van. Previously 082980. Converted on lot 3779, 1971. *Formerly SR BY S408S, to dia 3092 on RSCO A928 Ashford/Eastleigh 1937.*
ADB975142	QPV	Horsham. PSS Staff & Tool Brake Van. Converted on lot 3779, 1971. *Formerly SR BY S712S, to dia 3092 on RSCO A974 Ashford/Eastleigh 1938.*
ADB975143	QPV	Horsham. PSS Staff & Tool Brake Van. Previously 083004. *Formerly SR BY S405S, to dia 3092 on RSCO A928 Ashford/Eastleigh 1937.*
ADB975144	QTV	Horsham. PSS Tool Brake Van. Previously 083005. *Formerly SR BY S964S to dia 3092 on RSCO L1090 Lancing/Eastleigh 1940.*
RDB975146	QXV	RTC, Mickleover. Test Coach. *Formerly BR Mk1 CK M15239, to dia 126 on lot 30005 Metro-Cammell 1953.*
ADB975147	QQV	CF. BTU Tool Van. *Formerly BR Mk1 BSK W34841, to dia 182 on lot 30220 Gloucester 1956.*
ADB975148	QQV	LE. BTU Tool Van. OOU. *Formerly BR Mk1 BTK S34284, to dia 181 on lot 30021 Eastleigh 1952.*
ADB975150	QQV	Basingstoke. BTU Tool Van. OOU. *Formerly BR Mk1 BTK S34636, to dia 182 on lot 30143 Charles Roberts 1954.*
ADB975151	QQV	Basingstoke. BTU Tool Van. OOU. *Formerly BR Mk1 BTK W34874, to dia 182 on lot 30223 Charles Roberts 1956.*
ADB975157	QRV	ZL. Stores Van. *Formerly GWR (Collett) design BG W184W, to dia K41 on lot 1535 Swindon 1953.*
ADB975158	QRV	ZL. Stores Van. *Formerly GWR (Collett) design BG W185W, to dia K41 on lot 1535 Swindon 1953.*
ADB975161	QQV	BS. BTU Tool Van. Converted on lot 3785, 1972 to replace DM395382. *Formerly BR Mk1 TK M24070, to dia 146 on lot 30002 Derby 1951.*
ADB975162	QQV	WN. BTU Tool Van. Converted on lot 3785, 1972 to replace DM395479. *Formerly BR Mk1 TK M24157, to dia 146 on lot 30002 Derby 1951.*
TDB975177	QRV	Reading West Jct Yard. Stores Van. *Formerly GWR design Fruit D W3461W to dia Y11 on lot 1780 Swindon 1955.*
ADB975191	QPV	ED. BTU Staff Coach. Converted on lot 3789, 1972. *Formerly BR Mk1 BTO M9205, to dia 183 on lot 30170 Doncaster 1955.*
ADB975197	QRV	DY. RM & EE Class ISO Spares Stores Coach. Converted on lot 3797, 1972 for Prototype HST Vehicles. *Formerly BR Mk1 BTK E34375, to dia 181 on lot 30032 Wolverton 1952.*
ADB975198	QRV	DY. RM & EE Class 150 Spares Stores Coach. Converted on lot 3797, 1972 for Prototype HST Vehicles. *Formerly BR Mk1 BTK E34609, to dia 181 on lot 30141 Gloucester 1955.*
DB975199	QPV	ER. RCE Staff & Dormitory Coach for Ballast Cleaner DR76212. Converted on lot 3809, 1972 as prototype vehicle. *Formerly BR Mk1 BCK W21160, to dia 172 on lot 30187 Charles Roberts 1956.*
DB975200	QPV	ER. RCE Staff & Dormitory Coach for Ballast Cleaner DR76306. Converted on lot 3810, 1972 as prototype vehicle. *Formerly BR Mk1 BCK W21176, to dia 172 on lot 30424 Charles Roberts 1958.*
TDB975202	QVV	ST. Severn Tunnel Emergency Casualty Coach. *Formerly BR Mk1 BTK E34379, to dia 181 on lot 30032 Wolverton 1952.*
TDB975204*	QSO	Windsor Bridge, Manchester. Two Tier Car Loading Ramp. OOU. *Formerly BR Mk1 BTK, to dia 181 on lot 30021 Eastleigh 1951.*
TDB975205*	QSO	Luton Freight Sidings. Two Tier Car Loading Ramp. OOU. *Formerly BR Mk1 BTK, to dia 181 on lot 30021 Eastleigh 1951.*
DB975210	QPV	Slateford Engineers' Yard. RCE Staff Coach. Converted on lot 3793, 1972. *Formerly BR Mk1 BCK SC21019, to dia 171 on lot 30006 Metro-Cammell 1954.*
ADB975220	QPV	BR. BTU Staff & Dormitory Coach. Converted on lot 3795, 1972. *Formerly BR Mk1 BTK E34170, to dia 181 on lot 30025 Wolverton 1951.*

TDB975227 QWV LMR. Route Learning Car.
Formerly Class 122 DMBS M55017, to dia 539 on lot 30419 Gloucester 1958.

ADB975241 QQV AY. BTU Tool Van.
Formerly LMS GUV M37882M, to dia 1870 on lot 864 Wolverton 1935.

The following were converted from BR MK1 TKs to dia 146 (147*) on lot 3804 1972 to crane runners (QSB):

No.	*Crane*	*Location*	*Formerly*	*Build Details*		
DB975243	DRC81319	Beighton Engineers' Yard	SC24297	Lot 30026	York	1951
DB975244	DRC81337	Beighton Engineers' Yard	M25153*	Lot 30155	Wolverton	1956
DB975245	DRC81322	Crofton Engineers' Yard	SC24667	Lot 30057	B.R.C.W.	1953
DB975246	DRC81363	Crofton Engineers' Yard	SC24729	Lot 30073	Wolverton	1953
DB975247	DRC81373	Castleton CMD	SC24558	Lot 30044	York	1952
DB975248	DRC81320	Beighton Engineers' Yard	SC24658	Lot 30056	B.R.C.W.	1953

ADB975250 EZ5Q SG. RM & EE Stores Unit (931) 024. Converted 1973.
Formerly 4-Sub DMBSO S10829S, to dia 126 on lot 3384, 1948.

ADB975251 EZ5Q SG. RM & EE Stores Unit (931) 024. Converted 1973.
Formerly 4-Sub DMBSO S10830S, to dia 126 on lot 3384, 1948.

ADB975261 QXV Romford OHLM Depot. RM & EE OHLM Stores Van. Converted on lot 3812, 1973 to replace DE1570.
Formerly BR Mk1 TSO E4681, to dia 93 on lot 30375 York 1957.

ADB975262 QXV Romford OHLM Depot. RM & EE OHLM Staff Coach. Converted on lot 3812, 1973 to replace DE320698.
Formerly BR Mk1 BTK E34343, to dia 181 on lot 30075 Wolverton 1954.

ADB975277 QRV New Cross Gate C&W Shops. RM & EE Stores Van.
Formerly SR PMV S1938S, to dia 3103 on RSCO A973 Ashford 1938.

ADB975278 QXV RTC, Derby. Laboratory Coach 15, APT Catering Vehicle Mock Up.
Formerly BR Mk1 (1957 Prototype) FO W3082, to dia 76 on lot 30361 Cravens 1956.

RDB975280 QXA RTC, Derby. Laboratory Coach 18 'Mercury'. Converted on lot 3843, 1973.
Formerly BR Mk1 BCK S21263, to dia 172 on lot 30732 Derby 1964.

ADB975281 QWV (Cocklebury Sidings, Swindon). RM & EE Instruction Coach. Converted on lot 3817, 1973.
Formerly BR Mk1 BTO E9243, to dia 183 on lot 30170 Doncaster 1955.

KDB975282 QTV (New Cross Gate C&W Shops). S&T Brake Van.
Formerly SR BY S434S, to dia 3092 on RSCO A928 Ashford/Eastleigh 1937.

ADB975283 QPV Horsham. PSS Staff & Tool Brake Van.
Formerly SR BY S700S, to dia 3092 on RSCO A974 Ashford/Eastleigh 1938.

KDB975284 QTV (New Cross Gate C&W Shops). S&T Brake Van.
Formerly SR BY S764S, to dia 3092 on RSCO A1030 Ashford/Eastleigh 1939.

KDB975289 QPV Westbury. S&T Staff & Tool Coach.
Formerly BR Mk1 BTK W34620, to dia 182 on lot 30142 Gloucester 1955.

ADB975290 QXA RTC, Derby. M & EE Test Car 6. Converted on lot 3787.
Formerly BR Mk2 FK S13396, to dia 120 on lot 30734 Derby 1964.

KDB975291 QQV Reading RCE Plant Yard. S&T Tool Van.
Formerly Fruit C W2424W.

ADB975296 QSV Romford OHLM Depot. Runner for Crane ADRT96310. Converted on lot 3829, 1973.
Formerly BR Mk1 BTK E34480, to dia 181 on lot 30060 Gloucester 1953.

ADB975308 QQV HA. BTU Tool Van. Converted on lot 3835, 1973 to replace DE321044.
Formerly LNER Gresley BGP E70503E to dia 245 York 1938 (originally 5277).

RDB975311 QXO RTC, Derby. Soil Mechanics Stores Van.
Formerly SR BY S423S, to dia 3092 on RSCO A928 Ashford/Eastleigh 1937.

TDB975315 QXV York Up Yard. Operating Department Instruction Coach, 'TOPS HR3'.
Formerly BR Mk1 FO E3079, to dia 73 on lot 30242 Doncaster 1956.

ADB975319 EZ5F SR. RM & EE Instruction Coach, Unit (933) 055. Converted on lot 3838, 1973.
Formerly 4-Sub DMBS S10919S, to dia 119 on RSCO E3231 Eastleigh 1947.

ADB975320	EZ5C	SR. RM & EE Instruction Coach, Unit (933) 055. Converted on lot 3838, 1973. *Formerly 4-Sub Augmentation TS S10171S.*
ADB975321	EZ5C	SR. RM & EE Instruction Coach, Unit (933) 055. Converted on lot 3838, 1973. *Formerly 4-Sub TS (built as composite) S11470S.*
ADB975322	EZ5F	SR. RM & EE Instruction Coach, Unit (933) 055. Converted on lot 3838, 1973. *Formerly 4-Sub DMBS S10920S, to dia 119 on RSCO E3231 Eastleigh 1947.*
TDB975323	QXV	York Yard. Catering Instruction Coach. OOU. Converted on lot 3839, 1973. *Formerly BR Mk1 RSO W1013, to dia 56 on lot 30014 York 1951.*
TDB975324	QXV	(Bedford Engineers' Sidings). Catering Instruction Coach. OOU. Converted on lot 3839, 1973. *Formerly BR Mk1 RU W1901, to dia 23 on lot 30401 Swindon 1957.*
ADB975325	QXA	OO. M & EE Generator Van. *Formerly BR Mk1 BG M81448, to dia 711 on lot 30400 Pressed Steel 1957.*
DB975327	QPV	WR. RCE Staff and Dormitory Coach for Rail Profiler DX79105. *Formerly Class 123 TSLRB W59828, to dia 181 on lot 30705 Swindon 1963.*
ADB975329	ZQV	FH. BTU Tool Van. *Formerly BR Fish Van E88038, to dia 800 on lot 30442 Faverdale 1961.*
DB975336	QPV	Bristol Division. RCE Staff & Dormitory Van for Crane DRP81523. *Formerly BR (GWR design) Fruit D W92061, to dia 805 on lot 30345 Swindon 1958.*
DB975349	QWV	NL. RCE Inspection Saloon, coupled with DB975539. *Formerly Class 100 DMBS E51116, to dia 536 on lot 30444 Gloucester 1957.*
ADB975350	ZQV	IM. BTU Tool Van. *Formerly BR Fish Van E87612, to dia 800 on lot 30344 Faverdale 1960.*
ADB975375	QXV	(WD). RM & EE Instruction Coach. Previously 082232. *Formerly Bulleid S2526S.*
ADB975376	ZQV	FH. BTU Tool Van. *Formerly BR Fish Van E87872, to dia 800 on lot 30384 Faverdale 1960.*
ADB975377	ZQV	TI. BTU Tool Van. *Formerly BR Fish Van E87582, to dia 800 on lot 30344 Faverdale 1960.*
ADB975378	ZQV	(York Wagon Works). BTU Tool Van. *Formerly BR Fish Van E87601, to dia 800 on lot 30344 Faverdale 1960.*
DB975379	QPV	ER. RCE Staff & Dormitory Coach. Converted on lot 3851, 1975. *Formerly BR Mk1 TK E24982, to dia 531 on lot 30208 Derby 1956.*
DB975380	QPA	Liverpool. RCE Staff Van. Converted on lot 3854, 1976. *Formerly LMS PIII BG M31158M, to dia 2007 on lot 1304 Derby 1952.*
RDB975385	QWV	RTC, Derby. Laboratory Coach 9 'HYDRA', Hydraulic Transmission. *Formerly DMPMV M55997, to dia 531 on lot 30418 Cravens 1958.*
ADB975386	QXA	RTC, Derby. Laboratory Coach 4 'Hastings'. *Formerly Class 201 TSRB S60750, to dia 678 on lot 30393, 1958.*
DB975392	QSX	LMR. Match Wagon for Ballast Cleaner DR76216. Converted on lot 3862, 1974. *Formerly BT Mk1 TK M24308, to dia 147 on lot 30020 Eastleigh 1952.*
DB975393	QSX	WR. Match Wagon for Ballast Cleaner DR76215. Converted on lot 3862, 1974. *Formerly BT Mk1 CK M15474, to dia 126 on lot 30062 Metro-Cammell 1974.*
ADB975397	QXX	RTC, Derby. M & EE Test Car 2. Converted on lot 3894, 1977. *Formerly BT Mk1 BSK M35386, to dia 181 on lot 30699 Wolverton 1962.*
ZDB975403	QXX	ZN, operates on every region. Cinema Coach. Converted on lot 3865, 1975. *Formerly BT Mk1 TTO E4598, to dia 93 on lot 30243 York 1956.*
DB975411	QPV	Reading Division. RCE Staff & Dormitory Van for Crane DRP81509. Originally converted as Stores Van DB975382. *Formerly B.R. (GWR design) Fruit D W3465W to dia Y11 on lot 1780 Swindon 1955.*

The following are match wagons for ballast cleaners (QSB) and were converted on lot 3875, 1975 (975413-6) and lot 3876, 1975 (975412/7):

No.	Ballast Cleaner	Location	Formerly	Type	Dia	Build Details		
DB975412	DR76104	ER	M24485	TK	146	Lot 30070	Wolverton	1954
DB975413	DR76217	LMR	M15202	CK	126	Lot 30005	Metro-Cammell	1952
DB975414	DR76218	WR	E34499	BTK	181	Lot 30060	Gloucester	1953
DB975415	DR76219	LMR	E24011	TK	146	Lot 30002	Derby	1951
DB975416	DR76220	ScR	E34598	BTK	181	Lot 30141	Gloucester	1955
DB975417	DR76105	Connington, OOU.	E34498	BTK	181	Lot 30060	Gloucester	1953

ADB975419 ZQV TI. BTU Tool Van.
Formerly BR Fish Van E87885, to dia 800 on lot 30384 Faverdale 1960.

RDB975421 QXV RTC, Mickleover. Laboratory Coach 13.
Formerly BR Mk1 BTK M34068, to dia 181 on lot 30003 Derby 1952.

RDB975422 QXB RTC, Derby. Test Coach 'Prometheus'. Converted on lot 3910, 1976.
Formerly BR Mk1 BTK W34875, to dia 182 on lot 30223 Charles Roberts 1956.

ADB975423 QRV LN. RM & EE Stores Van, Asbestos Removal.
Formerly BR Fish Van E87910, to dia 800 on lot 30384 Faverdale 1960.

ADB975424 QPV (New Cross Gate C&W Shops). PSS Staff & Tool Van. Converted on lot 3877, 1974 to replace DW123036.
Formerly SR PMV S1107S, to dia 3103 on RSCO A855 Ashford 1936.

RDB975427 QXX RTC, Derby. Laboratory Coach 14 'Wren', Acoustics Section.
Formerly Pullman Kitchen First WREN (schedule 323) built Metro-Cammell 1960 (later BR M323E).

RDB975428 QXX RTC, Derby. Laboratory Coach 10.
Formerly BR Mk1 BTO M9236, to dia 183 on lot 30170 Doncaster 1955.

RDB975429 QRV RTC, Derby. Stores Coach.
Formerly BR Mk1 CK M15903, to dia 128 on lot 30222 Metro-Cammell 1956.

ADB975430 EZ5X RTC, Derby. M & EE Electricification Test Coach, Unit (920) 001. Converted on lot 3883, 1976.
Formerly BR MBSO ('PEP' Stock) S64300, to dia 861 on lot 30818, 1971.

ADB975431 EZ5V RTC, Derby. M & EE Electrification Test Coach, Unit (920) 001. Converted on lot 3883, 1976. New build vehicle to dia 477.

ADB975432 EZ5X RTC, Derby. M&EE Electrification Test Coach, Unit (920) 001. Converted on lot 3883 1976.
Formerly BR MBSO ('PEP' Stock) S64301, to dia 861 on lot 30818, 1971.

ADB975434 QPV CA. RM & EE Staff & Stores Coach.
Formerly BR Mk1 BTK E34731, to dia 181 on lot 30156 Wolverton 1955.

TDB975449 ZRV (TE). Severn Tunnel Emergency Train Tank Wagon. OOU.
Formerly B.R. Milk Tank B3192, to dia O56 on lot 1760, 1952.

TDB975450‡ ZRV BJ. Severn Tunnel Emergency Train Tank Wagon. OOU.
Formerly B.R. (W.R.) Milk Tank W2021, to dia O56 on lot 1760, 1952.

TDB975451 ZRV BJ. Severn Tunnel Emergency Train Tank Wagon. OOU.
Formerly L.M.S. Milk Tank M44181, to dia 1994 on lot 631 Derby 1931.

TDB975452 ZRV BJ. Severn Tunnel Emergency Train Tank Wagon. OOU.
Formerly S.R. Milk Tank S4433S, to dia 3158 on RSCO. 828 1935.

The following vehicles were initially BTU staff, tool and generator coaches (QPX) converted on lot 3892 from BR Mk1 BTK/BSKs to dia 181 (182*); ADB975454/8 have been further converted to BTU tool vans and RDB975453/7 are to be similarly converted:

No.	Location	Formerly	Build Details		
ADB975453	CR	E34780*	Lot 30157	Wolverton	1955
ADB975454	DR	E35083	Lot 30233	Gloucester	1956
ADB975455	SB	E35087	Lot 30233	Gloucester	1956
ADB975456	NC	E35088	Lot 30233	Gloucester	1956
ADB975457	IM	E35085	Lot 30233	Gloucester	1956
ADB975458	SF	E34610	Lot 30141	Gloucester	1955
ADB975459	WN	M34136	Lot 30025	Wolverton	1951
ADB975460	BY	E34586	Lot 30141	Gloucester	1955
ADB975461	NH	E34153	Lot 30025	Wolverton	1951
ADB975462	BS	E35080	Lot 30233	Gloucester	1956

ADB975463 QPX (ZF for repair). BTU Staff, Tool and Dormitory Coach. Converted on lot 3891. *Formerly BR Mk1 BTK SC34721, to dia 181 on lot 30156 Wolverton 1955.*

ADB975464 QPX MR. BTU Staff, Tool and Dormitory Coach. Converted on lot 3891. *Formerly BR Mk1 BSK E35171, to dia 181 on lot 30386 Charles Roberts 1957.*

The following vehicles are all BTU staff and tool coaches (QPX) converted on lot 3891 from BR Mk1 BTK/BSKs to dia 181:

No.	*Location*	*Formerly*	*Build Details*		
ADB975465	TO	E35109	Lot 30233	Gloucester	1956
ADB975466	(Stratford Repair Depot)	E35094	Lot 30233	Gloucester	1956
ADB975467	ML	SC35271	Lot 30427	Gloucester	1957
ADB975468	EH	M34553	Lot 30095	Wolverton	1955
ADB975469	Stratford Repair Depot	E35090	Lot 30233	Gloucester	1956
ADB975470	TI	M34527	Lot 30095	Wolverton	1955
ADB975471	WN	M34543	Lot 30095	Wolverton	1955
ADB975472	CF	E35079	Lot 30233	Gloucester	1956
ADB975473	BR	E35086	Lot 30233	Gloucester	1956
ADB975475	OC	M34369	Lot 30074	Wolverton	1954
ADB975476	TE	M34368	Lot 30074	Wolverton	1954
ADB975477	SP	E35108	Lot 30233	Gloucester	1956
ADB975478	Perth Station Sidings	E35173	Lot 30386	Charles Roberts	1957
ADB975479	(Carlisle Currock C&W Shops)	M34364	Lot 30074	Wolverton	1954
ADB975480	IS	M34585	Lot 30141	Gloucester	1955

The following vehicles are all BTU tool and generator vans (QQX) converted on lot 3893 from BR Mk1 BTK/BSKs to dia 181:

No.	*Location*	*Formerly*	*Build Details*		
ADB975481	TO	E34606	Lot 30141	Gloucester	1955
ADB975482	GD	E34602	Lot 30141	Gloucester	1955
ADB975483	HA	E35104	Lot 30233	Gloucester	1956
ADB975484	EH	E34591	Lot 30141	Gloucester	1955
ADB975485	BR	E34594	Lot 30141	Gloucester	1955
ADB975486	FH	E35100	Lot 30233	Gloucester	1956
ADB975487	SF	E35092	Lot 30233	Gloucester	1956
ADB975488	TI	E35099	Lot 30233	Gloucester	1956
ADB975489	DR	E34786	Lot 30157	Wolverton	1955
ADB975490	(Rugby C&W Shops)	E34746	Lot 30156	Wolverton	1955
ADB975491	HM	E35096	Lot 30233	Gloucester	1956
ADB975492	ML	E34589	Lot 30141	Gloucester	1955
ADB975493	BS	E34740	Lot 30156	Wolverton	1955
ADB975494	OC	E35082	Lot 30233	Gloucester	1956
ADB975495	SP	E35093	Lot 30233	Gloucester	1956
ADB975496	KD	M34004	Lot 30003	Derby	1951
ADB975497	CF	E35218	Lot 30427	Wolverton	1957
ADB975498	GD	M34367	Lot 30074	Wolverton	1954
ADB975499	(ZF for repair)	M34365	Lot 30074	Wolverton	1954

The following RCE Long Welded Rail Carriers were converted on lot 3717 1970. All are based at Redbridge RCE Depot, Southampton.

'MANTA' CARKIND YKA

DB975500 Formerly S12274S, 6-Pan TFK to dia 2506
DB975501 Formerly S12265S, 6-Pan TFK to dia 2506
DB975502 Formerly S12262S, 6-Pan TFK to dia 2506
DB975503 Formerly S12263S, 6-Pan TFK to dia 2506
DB975504 Formerly S12268S, 6-Pan TFK to dia 2506
DB975505 Formerly S12269S, 6-Pan TFK to dia 2506
DB975506 Formerly S12267S, 6-Pan TFK to dia 2506
DB975507 Formerly S12273S, 6-Pan TFK to dia 2506

'MARLIN' CARKIND YKA

DB975508 Formerly S10039S, 4-Cor TSK
DB975509 Formerly S10040S, 4-Cor TSK
DB975510 Formerly S10032S, 4-Cor TSK
DB975511 Formerly S10037S, 4-Cor TSK

DB975512 Formerly S10035S, 4-Cor TSK
DB975513 Formerly S10048S, 4-Cor TSK
DB975514 Formerly S10050S, 4-Cor TSK
DB975515 Formerly S10049S, 4-Cor TSK
DB975516 Formerly S10025S, 4-Cor TSK
DB975517 Formerly S10036S, 4-Cor TSK
DB975518 Formerly S10026S, 4-Cor TSK
DB975519 Formerly S10081S, 4-Buf TCK
DB975520 Formerly S11847S, 4-Cor TCK
DB975521 Formerly S11846S, 4-Cor TCK
DB975522 Formerly S11849S, 4-Cor TCK
DB975523 Formerly S11856S, 4-Cor TCK
DB975524 Formerly S11817S, 4-Res TFK
DB975525 Formerly S11854S, 4-Buf TCK
DB975526 Formerly S10064S, 4-Cor TSK
DB975527 Formerly S11800S, 4-Res TFK
DB975528 Formerly S12245S, 4-Res TFK
DB975529 Formerly S10079S, 4-Cor TSK
DB975530 Formerly S11815S, 4-Cor TCK
DB975531 Formerly S11802S, 4-Cor TCK
DB975532 Formerly S10103S, 4-Cor TSK
DB975533 Formerly S10041S, 6-Pan TSK

DB975534 QPV All Regions. RCE Staff, Dormitory & Workshop Coach for Viaduct Inspection Unit DR82100. Converted on lot 3719, 1970 for Soil Mechanics Section.
Formerly BR Mk1 BTK S34255, to dia 181 on lot 30021 Eastleigh 1951.

DB975535 QPV Wimbledon Engineers' Yard, operates on every Region. Soil Mechanics' Section Staff, Dormitory & Tool Coach. Converted on lot 3719, 1970.
Formerly BR Mk1 BTK S34259, to dia 181 on lot 30021 Eastleigh 1951.

TDB975536 QSV Bescot Yard. Two-Tier Car Loading Ramp. OOU. Converted on lot 3721, 1970 for Stirling.
Formerly BR Mk1 CK Sc15165, to dia 126 on lot 30005 Metro-Cammell 1952.

ADB975537 QQV ED. BTU Tool Van. Converted on lot 3737, 1970 from Stores Van DE321132.
Formerly LNER BGP E70495E, to dia 245 York 1940 (originally 4272).

DB975538 QPV LMR. RCE Staff & Dormitory Portakabin Vehicle for Twin Jib Crane DRB78113. Converted as prototype vehicle (further conversions cancelled).
Formerly BR Mk1 BTK W34778, to dia 182 on lot 30157 Wolverton 1955.

DB975539 QWV NL. RCE Inspection Saloon, coupled with DB975349. Converted on lot 3923, 1977.
Formerly Class 100 DTCL E56101, to dia 537 on lot 30279 Gloucester 1957.

TDB975540 QWV RG. Route Learning Car.
Formerly Class 122 DMBS W55016, to dia 539 on lot 30419 Gloucester 1958.

ADB975546 QVV Rugby OHLM Depot. RM & EE OHLM Cable Drum Carrier. Converted on lot 3897, 1976.
Formerly BR Mk1 TK M24589, to dia 146 on lot 30057 BRCW 1953.

RDB975547 QXA RTC, Derby. Laboratory Coach 23. RTC, Derby.
Formerly BR Mk1 BG M81617, to dia 711 on lot 30725 Gloucester 1962.

ADB975548 QSW SR. Match for Single Buffer Electric Stock.
Formerly SR BY S419S, to dia 3092 on RSCO A928 Ashford/Eastleigh 1937.

ADB975550 QRX HE. RM & EE OHLM Stores Coach. Converted on lot 3898, 1976.
Formerly BR Mk1 BSK E35141, to dia 181 on lot 30386 Charles Roberts 1957.

ADB975551 QXX HE. RM & EE OHLM Pantograph Coach. Converted on lot 3899, 1976.
Formerly BR Mk1 BSK M35133, to dia 181 on lot 30386 Charles Roberts 1957.

ADB975552 QXX HE. RM & EE OHLM Pantograph Coach. Converted on lot 3899, 1976.
Formerly BR Mk1 BSK E35137, to dia 181 on lot 30386 Charles Roberts 1957.

ADB975553 QXX HE. RM & EE OHLM Stores & Generator Coach. Converted on lot 3900, 1976.
Formerly BR Mk1 BSK E35230, to dia 181 on lot 30427 Wolverton 1957.

ADB975554 QXX HE. RM & EE OHLM Stores & Roof Access Coach. Converted on lot 3901, 1976.
Formerly BR Mk1 BSK E35175, to dia 181 on lot 30386 Charles Roberts 1957.

ADB975555	QPX	HE. RM & EE OHLM Staff & Office Coach. Converted on lot 3902, 1976. *Formerly BR Mk1 BSK E35164, to dia 181 on lot 30386 Charles Roberts 1957.*
ADB975557	QXX	GW. RM & EE OHLM Pantograph Coach. Converted on lot 3904, 1976. *Formerly BR Mk1 BSK E35232, to dia 181 on lot 30427 Wolverton 1957.*
ADB975558	QXX	GW. RM & EE OHLM Stores & Generator Coach. Converted on lot 3905, 1976. *Formerly BR Mk1 BSK E35263, to dia 181 on lot 30427 Wolverton 1957.*
ADB975559	QPX	GW. RM & EE OHLM Staff & Office Coach. Converted on lot 3906, 1976. *Formerly BR Mk1 BSK E35211, to dia 181 on lot 30427 Wolverton 1957.*
ADB975560	QRV	AB. RM & EE Stores Van. *Formerly LMS GUV M37909M, to dia 1870 on lot 1050 Wolverton 1937.*
ADB975562	QRV	Crewe South Yard. RM & EE Stores Van, 'ENPARTS'. OOU. *Formerly LMS PIII BG M30976M, to dia 2007 on lot 1096 Wolverton 1938.*
DB975563	QPA	ER. RCE Staff & Dormitory Van for Twin Jib Crane DRP78220. *Formerly SR design PMV S1476S, to dia 3103 built Wolverton 1951.*
DB975565	QPB	ER. RCE Staff & Dormitory Van for Tecfer Track Relayer 78345. *Formerly SR design PMV S1647S, to dia 3103 on RSCO A3590 Ashford/Lancing 1950.*
DB975566	QQA	SR. RCE Tool Van. *Formerly SR design PMV S1496S, to dia 3103 built Wolverton 1951.*
DB975568	QPA	WR. RCE Staff & Dormitory Van. *Formerly SR design PMV S1626S, to dia 3103 on RSCO A3590 Ashford/Lancing 1950.*
KDB975571	QPV	Bedford Engineers' Sidings. S&T Dormitory Coach. *Formerly LMS design PIII SLT(T) M614M, to dia 2169 on lot 1628 Derby 1952.*
ADB975573	QPV	(Cocklebury Sidings, Swindon). BTU Staff & Dormitory Coach. Converted on lot 3912, 1976. Carried ADB975480 in error. *Formerly BR Mk1 BTK E34729, to dia 181 on lot 30156 Wolverton 1955.*
ADB975574	QPV	(ZY for repair). BTU Staff Coach. Converted on lot 3913, 1976. Carried ADB975481 in error. *Formerly BR Mk1 BTK E34599, to dia 181 on lot 30141 Gloucester 1955.*
ADB975576	QRV	EC. RM & EE Stores Van. Converted 1977. *Formerly LNER (Thompson) BG E11E, to dia 344 on lot 1180 York 1947. Built for Flying Scotsman Service.*
DB975581	QPV	(FW). Glasgow North RCE Dormitory Coach. Converted 1977. *Formerly LMS PIII SLT(T) M613M, to dia 2169 on lot 1628 Derby 1952.*
DB975583	QPV	(Crianlarich Upper). Glasgow North RCE Dormitory Coach. Converted 1977. *Formerly LMS PIII SLT(T) M620M, to dia 2169 on lot 1628 Derby 1952.*

The following RM & EE De-Icing Units were converted on lot 3915, 1976 from former 4-Sub DMBS, to dia 119 on RSCO E3231 Eastleigh 1947 (975586/7, 604/5), 4-Sub DMBSO, to dia 119 on RSCO E1060 Eastleigh 1941 (975588/9/92/5/7-600/2/3), 4-Sub DMBSO, to dia 119 on RSCO E3384 Eastleigh 1948 (975590/1/6, 601), 4-Sub DMBSO, to dia 119 on RSCO E3618 Eastleigh 1950 (975593/4).

All are EZ5D, Units (930)...

ADB975586	Formerly S10907S	004 AF
ADB975587	Formerly S10908S	004 AF
ADB975588	Formerly S10981S	005 WD
ADB975589	Formerly S10982S	005 WD
ADB975590	Formerly S10833S	006 BI
ADB975591	Formerly S10834S	006 BI
ADB975592	Formerly S10993S	007 GI
ADB975593	Formerly S12659S	007 GI
ADB975594	Formerly S12658S	003 SU
ADB975595	Formerly S10994S	003 SU
ADB975596	Formerly S10844S	008 WD
ADB975597	Formerly S10987S	008 WD
ADB975598	Formerly S10989S	009 EH
ADB975599	Formerly S10990S	009 EH
ADB975600	Formerly S10988S	010 BI
ADB975601	Formerly S10843S	010 BI

ADB975602 Formerly S10991S 011 RE
ADB975603 Formerly S10992S 011 RE
ADB975604 Formerly S10939S 012 FR
ADB975605 Formerly S10940S 012 FR

RDB975606 QXA RTC, Mickleover. Laboratory Coach 2 'Electra'. Converted 1977.
Formerly BR Mk1 FO S3068, to dia 73 on lot 30169 Doncaster 1955.

ADB975607 QXA (ZD for repair). M & EE Test Car 7. Converted 1977.
Formerly BR Mk1 FO S3064, to dia 73 on lot 30169 Doncaster 1955.

ADB975610 QQX (Cardiff Cathays C&W Shops). BTU Tool Van. Provisionally destined for BR. Converted to Stores Van on lot 3917, 1976.
Formerly BR Mk1 BG M80942, to dia 711 on lot 30162 Pressed Steel 1957. Converted to TLV S68205.

ADB975611 QQX (Cardiff Cathays C&W Shops). BTU Tool Van. Provisionaly destined for OC. Converted to stores van on lot 3917, 1976.
Formerly BR Mk1 BG M80915, to dia 711 on lot 30162 Pressed Steel 1957. Converted to TLV S68201.

ADB975612 QQX (Cardiff Cathays C&W Shops). BTU Tool Van. Provisionally destined for CF. Converted to stores van on lot 3917, 1976.
Formerly BR Mk1 BG M80922, to dia 711 on lot 30162 Pressed Steel 1957. Converted to TLV S68203.

ADB975613 QQX OC. BTU Tool Van. Converted originally to stores van on lot 3917, 1976.
Formerly BR Mk1 BG S80918, to dia 711 on lot 30162, Pressed Steel 1957. Converted to TLV S68202.

ADB975614 QQX LE. BTU Tool Van. Converted originally to stores van on lot 3917, 1976.
Formerly BR Mk1 BG M80925, to dia 711 on lot 30162 Pressed Steel 1957. Converted to TLV S68204.

ADB975615 QQX BR. BTU Tool Van. Converted originally to stores van on lot 3917, 1976.
Formerly BR Mk1 BG M80951, to dia 711 on lot 30162 Pressed Steel 1957. Converted to TLV S68206

ADB975616 QPV ST. BTU Staff & Tool Coach. Converted 1977.
Formerly BR Mk1 BSK E35077, to dia 181 on lot 30233 Gloucester 1957.

ADB975618 QXV Basford Hall Yard, Crewe. ZC Test Train Coach. Converted 1977.
Formerly BR Mk1 BTK M34359, to dia 181 on lot 30074 Wolverton 1954.

ADB975626 QXV Basford Hall Yard, Crewe. ZC Test Train Coach. Converted 1977.
Formerly BR Mk1 BSK S34939, to dia 182 on lot 30229 Metro-Cammell 1956.

ADB975627 QXV Basford Hall Yard, Crewe. ZC Test Train Coach. Converted 1977.
Formerly BR Mk1 BSK S34938, to dia 182 on lot 30229 Metro-Cammell 1956.

CDB975629 QSV ZD. Barrier Coach, HST. OOU. Converted 1977.
Formerly BR Mk2a BFK M14084, to dia 163 on lot 30786 Derby 1968.

ADB975630 QXA RTC, Derby. M & EE Test Car 8. Converted 1977.
Formerly BR Mk1 FO W3011, to dia 72 on lot 30008 BRCW 1954.

ADB975631 QXA RTC. Derby. M & EE Test Car 9. Converted 1978.
Formerly BR Mk1 FO W3009, to dia 72 on lot 30008 BRCW 1954.

RDB975634 QXA RTC, Derby. Power Coach 'PC3', 3 coach articulated POP Train Unit. Built RTC.

RDB975635 QXA RTC, Derby. Power Coach 'PC4', 3 coach articulated POP Train Unit. Built RTC.

RDB975636 QXA RTC, Derby. Laboratory Coach 8, 3 coach articulated POP Train Unit. Built RTC.

DB975637 QWV NL. RCE Inspection Saloon, coupled with DB975664. Converted on lot 3923, 1977.
Formerly Class 100 DTCL E56300, to dia 537 on lot 30445 Gloucester 1957.

ADB975638 QPB Horsham. PSS Staff & Tool Coach. Converted from Stores Coach at SG on Lot 4039, 1983.
Formerly BR Mk1 BSK S34999, to dia 182 on lot 30229 Metro-Cammell 1956.

ADB975639 QQA WD. BTU Tool Van. Converted from Stores Coach at SG on Lot 4039, 1983. Previously IU083527.
Formerly BR Mk1 BSK S35016, to dia 182 on lot 30229 Metro-Cammell 1957.

ADB975640 QQV RG. BTU Tool Van. Converted 1977.
Formerly GWR (Hawksworth) BG W276W, to dia K42 on lot 1665 Swindon 1945.

DB975641 QPV ER. RCE Staff Coach for DR88XXX Skip Train. Converted 1977.
Formerly BR Mk1 BSO E9279, to dia 183 on lot 30244 Doncaster 1956.

ADB975642 QPV LN. Staff Changing Van. Converted 1977.
Formerly LNER design Fish Van E87247, to dia 800 on lot 30125 Faverdale 1954.

The following are HST barrier coaches (QSA) converted 1977/8 from BR Mk1s (975648/50-3/8) and Mk2a's (975654/5). They are mainly used on the Eastern and Scottish Regions:

No.	*Formerly*	*Type*	*Dia.*	*Build Details*	
ADB975648	E1052	RUO	61	Lot 30647 Wolverton	1961
ADB975650	E3016	FO	72	Lot 30008 B.R.C.W.	1954
ADB975651	S34964	BSK	182	Lot 30229 Metro-Cammell	1956
ADB975652	S34988	BSK	182	Lot 30229 Metro-Cammell	1956
ADB975653	E3013	FO	72	Lot 30008 B.R.C.W.	1954
ADB975654	W14067	BFK	163	Lot 30775 Derby	1967
ADB975655	W14065	BFK	163	Lot 30775 Derby	1967
ADB975658	E3014	FO	72	Lot 30008 B.R.C.W.	1954

DB975659 QWV RG. Route Learning Car. Converted on lot 3956, 1978.
Formerly Class 121 DMBS W55035, to dia 512 on lot 30518 Pressed Steel 1960.

ADB975660 QSA ER/ScR. HST Barrier Coach. Converted 1978.
Formerly BR Mk1 BSK S35006, to dia 182 on lot 30229 Metro-Cammell 1956.

KDB975661 QPV (EC). Staff & Dormitory Coach. Converted on lot 3931, 1978.
Formerly BR Mk1 BCK M21228, to dia 171 on lot 30474 Charles Roberts 1959.

KDB975662 QPV (Ladybank). S&T Staff & Dormitory Coach. Converted on lot 3931, 1978.
Formerly BR Mk1 BSK E35215, to dia 181 on lot 30427 Wolverton 1957.

DB975663 QXW SR(SED). RCE Tunnel Inspection Van, (with DS70164). Converted on lot 3933, 1978.
Formerly S.R. GUV S4593S, to dia 2182 on RSCO A975 Ashford/Eastleigh 1938.

DB975664 QWV NL. RCE Inspection Saloon, coupled with DB975637.
Formerly Class 100 DMBS E51122, to dia 536 on lot 30444 Gloucester 1957.

ADB975665 QSA WR. HST Barrier Coach. Converted 1978.
Formerly BR Mk2A BFK W14071, to dia 163 on lot 30775 Derby 1968.

ADB975666 QSA WR. HST Barrier Coach. Converted 1978.
Formerly BR Mk2A BFK W14078, to dia 163 on lot 30786 Derby 1968.

RDB975667 QRV RTC, Derby. Track Maintenance Equipment Stores Van. Converted 1978.
Formerly LMS CCT M37210M, to dia 2026 on GWR lot 1770 Swindon 1956.

TDB975668 QXV BJ. Severn Tunnel Emergency Casualty Van. OOU. Converted 1978.
Formerly GWR (Hawksworth) design BG W313W, to dia K45 on lot 1740 Swindon 1950.

DB975669 QPB SR. RCE Staff & Tool Van. Converted on lot 3934, 1978.
Formerly SR design PMV S1455S, to dia 3103 built Wolverton 1951.

DB975670 QPB SR. RCE Staff & Tool Van. Converted on lot 3934, 1978.
Formerly SR design PMV S1459S, to dia 3103 built Wolverton 1951.

ADB975672 QSW SR. Match for Single Buffer Electric Stock. Converted 1978.
Formerly SR BY S435S, to dia 3092 on RSCO A928 Ashford/Eastleigh 1937.

ADB975678 QSA WR. HST Barrier Coach. Converted 1978.
Formerly BR Mk1 BCK S21251, to dia 171 on lot 30669 Swindon 1962.

ADB975680 QXX GW. RM & EE OHLM Pantograph Coach. Converted on lot 3941, 1978.
Formerly BR Mk1 BSK E35160, to dia 181 on lot 30386 Charles Roberts 1957.

ADB975681 QXX Carstairs OHLM Depot. RM & EE OHLM Pantograph Coach. Converted on lot 3941, 1978.
Formerly BR Mk1 BTK W34781, to dia 182 on lot 30157 Wolverton 1955.

ADB975682 QXX Carstairs OHLM Depot. RM & EE OHLM Pantograph Coach. Converted on lot 3941, 1978.
Formerly BR Mk1 BTK M34467, to dia 181 on lot 30060 Gloucester 1953.

ADB975683 QRX GW. RM & EE OHLM Stores Coach. Converted on lot 3942, 1978.
Formerly BR Mk1 BSK E35252, to dia 181 on lot 30427 Wolverton 1957.

ADB975684 QRX GW. RM & EE OHLM Stores Coach. Converted on lot 3942, 1978.
Formerly BR Mk1 BSK E35140, to dia 181 on lot 30386 Charles Roberts 1957.

ADB975685 QXX Carstairs OHLM Depot. RM & EE OHLM Stores & Generator Van. Converted on lot 3943, 1978.
Formerly BR Mk1 TK E24662, to dia 146 on lot 30057 BRCW 1953.

ADB975686 QXX Carstairs OHLM Depot. RM & EE OHLM Stores & Roof Access Coach. Converted on lot 3944, 1978.
Formerly BR Mk1 CK M15971, to dia 126 on lot 30317 Wolverton 1956.

ADB975687 QXX Carstairs OHLM Depot. RM & EE OHLM Stores and Roof Access Coach. Converted on lot 3944, 1978.
Formerly BR Mk1 CK E15846, to dia 126 on lot 30221 Metro-Cammell 1956.

ADB975688 QPX Carstairs OHLM Depot. RM & EE OHLM Staff & Office Coach. Converted on lot 3945, 1978.
Formerly BR Mk1 CK E15764, to dia 126 on lot 30179 Metro-Cammell 1955.

The following vehicles are RM & EE OHLM pantograph coaches (QXX) converted on lot 3946 1978 from BR Mk1 BTK/BSKs to diagram 181 (except 975702-4 which were converted from BCKs to diagrams 171 and 172 and a BTO to diagram 183 respectively).

No.	*Location*	*Formerly*	*Build Details*	
ADB975689	CL	E35236	Lot 30427 Wolverton	1957
ADB975690	CL	E35157	Lot 30386 Charles Roberts	1957
ADB975691	CE	E35227	Lot 30427 Wolverton	1957
ADB975692	CE	E35214	Lot 30427 Wolverton	1957
ADB975693	BE	M34363	Lot 30074 Wolverton	1954
ADB975694	BE	M34522	Lot 30095 Wolverton	1955
ADB975695	LG	E35097	Lot 30233 Gloucester	1956
ADB975696	LG	E35081	Lot 30233 Gloucester	1956
ADB975697	SP	M34147	Lot 30025 Wolverton	1951
ADB975698	SP	M34148	Lot 30025 Wolverton	1951
ADB975699	Salop Sidings, Stafford	M35105	Lot 30233 Gloucester	1956
ADB975700	Salop Sidings, Stafford	M34138	Lot 30025 Wolverton	1951
ADB975701	SI	M34085	Lot 30003 Derby	1951
ADB975702	SI	E21108	Lot 30185 Metro-Cammell	1956
ADB975703	Rugby OHLM Depot	SC21182	Lot 30424 Charles Roberts	1958
ADB975704	Rugby OHLM Depot	SC9270	Lot 30170 Doncaster	1955
ADB975705	BY	E34534	Lot 30095 Wolverton	1955
ADB975706	BY	E34655	Lot 30156 Wolverton	1955
ADB975707	WN	M34541	Lot 30095 Wolverton	1955
ADB975708	WN	M35041	Lot 30233 Gloucester	1956

The following vehicles are RM & EE OHLM stores coaches (QRX) converted on lot 3947, 1978 from BR Mk1 BSKs to diagram 181 (975709/10), SKs to diagram 146 (975711-4) and TTO/TSOs to dia 93 (975715-8). Note: 975711 was converted on lot 3990, 1981.

No.	*Location*	*Formerly*	*Build Details*	
ADB975709	CL	E35268	Lot 30427 Wolverton	1957
ADB975710	CL	E35221	Lot 30427 Wolverton	1957
ADB975711	BE	E25434	Lot 30350 Wolverton	1957
ADB975712	LG	M25262	Lot 30349 Wolverton	1957
ADB975713	SP	E25420	Lot 30350 Wolverton	1957
ADB975714	Salop Sidings, Stafford	M25466	Lot 30374 York	1958
ADB975715	SI	M3955	Lot 30086 Eastleigh	1954
ADB975716	Rugby OHLM Depot	E4587	Lot 30243 York	1956
ADB975717	BY	E4559	Lot 30243 York	1956
ADB975718	WN	E4645	Lot 30375 York	1957

The following vehicles are RM & EE OHLM stores & generator vans (QXX) converted on lot 3948, 1978 from BR Mk1 BSKs to dia 181 (975719-20), SKs to dia 146 (975721-3) & CK to dia 126 (975724) and TSOs to dia 93 (975725/7/8). 975726 was a BR Mk1 TK and was originally converted as a staff coach ADB975979 for Ripple Lane C&W. Note: 975721 was converted on lot 3991, 1981.

No.	*Location*	*Formerly*	*Build Details*	
ADB975719	CL	E35266	Lot 30427 Wolverton	1957
ADB975720	CL	E35165	Lot 30386 Charles Roberts	1957
ADB975721	BE	M25600	Lot 30426 Wolverton	1957
ADB975722	LG	E25226	Lot 30230 Metro-Cammell	1957
ADB975723	SP	E25388	Lot 30349 Wolverton	1957
ADB975724	Salop Sidings, Stafford	M16079	Lot 30471 Metro-Cammell	1958
ADB975725	SI	E4581	Lot 30243 York	1956
ADB975726	Rugby OHLM Depot	E24531	Lot 30070 York	1954
ADB975727	BY	E4348	Lot 30207 BRCW	1956
ADB975728	WN	E4693	Lot 30375 York	1957

The following vehicles are RM & EE OHLM stores & roof access coaches (QXX) converted on lot 3949 from BR Mk1 BSKs to dia 181 (975729/30), SK/TKs to dia 146 (975731/2/4/6/8), a CK to dia 126 (975733) and TTO/TSOs to dia 93 (975735/7). Note: 975731 was converted on lot 3992, 1981.

No.	*Location*	*Formerly*	*Build Details*	
ADB975729	CL	E35253	Lot 30427 Wolverton	1957
ADB975730	CE	E35163	Lot 30386 Charles Roberts	1957
ADB975731	BE	E25674	Lot 30426 Wolverton	1957
ADB975732	LG	E24766	Lot 30078 Swindon	1960
ADB975733	SP	E16001	Lot 30351 Wolverton	1956
ADB975734	Salop Sidings, Stafford	M25695	Lot 30426 Wolverton	1957
ADB975735	SI	M3974	Lot 30090 York	1954
ADB975736	Rugby OHLM Depot	E25190	Lot 30230 Metro-Cammell	1957
ADB975737	BY	E4395	Lot 30219 Swindon	1957
ADB975738	WN	E25479	Lot 30374 York	1958

The following vehicles are RM & EE OHLM staff & office coaches (QPX) converted on lot 3950, 1978 from BR Mk1 BSKs to dia 181 (975739/40) SKs to dia 146 (975741-4) TSOs to dia 93 (975745-8). Note: 975741 was converted on lot 3993, 1981.

No.	*Location*	*Formerly*	*Build Details*	
ADB975739	CL	E35154	Lot 30386 Charles Roberts	1957
ADB975740	CE	E35132	Lot 30386 Charles Roberts	1957
ADB975741	BE	M25664	Lot 30426 Wolverton	1957
ADB975742	LG	E25017	Lot 30208 Derby	1956
ADB975743	SP	E25358	Lot 30349 Wolverton	1957
ADB975744	Salop Sidings, Stafford	M25440	Lot 30350 Wolverton	1957
ADB975745	SI	E4283	Lot 30207 BRCW	1956
ADB975746	Rugby OHLM Depot	E4343	Lot 30207 BRCW	1956
ADB975747	BY	E4351	Lot 30207 BRCW	1956
ADB975748	WN	E4652	Lot 30375 York	1957

The following vehicles are RM & EE OHLM pantograph coaches (QXX) converted on lot 3951, 1978 from BR Mk1 BSKs to dia 181 except 975750 which was a BFK to dia 161.

ADB975749	Romford OHLM Depot	E35138	Lot 30386 Charles Roberts	1957
ADB975750	Romford OHLM Depot	M14011	Lot 30382 Swindon	1960
ADB975751	Romford OHLM Depot	M34362	Lot 30074 Wolverton	1954
ADB975752	Romford OHLM Depot	M34568	Lot 30095 Wolverton	1955
ADB975753	Romford OHLM Depot	E35441	Lot 30721 Wolverton	1963
ADB975754	Romford OHLM Depot	E35347	Lot 30699 Wolverton	1962

ADB975757 QRX Romford OHLM Depot. RM & EE Stores Coach. Converted on lot 3952 1978.
Formerly BR Mk1 BSK E35265 to dia 181 on lot 30427 Wolverton, 1957.

ADB975758 QRX Romford OHLM Depot. RM & EE Stores Coach. Converted on lot 3952 1978.
Formerly BR Mk1 SK M25430 to dia 146 on lot 30350 Wolverton 1957.

ADB975759 QRX Romford OHLM Depot. RM & EE Stores Coach. Converted on lot 3952 1978.
Formerly BR Mk1 SK E25495 to dia 146 on lot 30374 York 1958.

The following vehicles are RM & EE OHLM stores and generator coaches (QXX) converted on lot 3953, 1978 from BR Mk1 SKs to dia 146, except 975761 which was a BSK to dia 181.

No.	Location	Formerly	Build Details	
ADB975761	Romford OHLM Depot	E35273	Lot 30427 Wolverton	1957
ADB975762	Romford OHLM Depot	M25437	Lot 30350 Wolverton	1957
ADB975763	Romford OHLM Depot	M25353	Lot 30349 Wolverton	1957

ADB975765 QXX Romford OHLM Depot. RM & EE OHLM Stores & Roof Access Coach. Converted on lot 3954, 1978.
Formerly BR Mk1 BSK E35170, to dia 181 on lot 30386 Charles Roberts 1957.

ADB975766 QXX Romford OHLM Depot. RM & EE OHLM Stores & Roof Access Coach. Converted on lot 3954, 1978.
Formerly BR Mk1 SK E25477, to dia 146 on lot 30374 York 1958.

ADB975767 QXX Romford OHLM Depot. RM & EE OHLM Stores & Roof Access Coach. Converted on lot 3954, 1978.
Formerly BR Mk1 SK E25641, to dia 146 on lot 30426 Wolverton 1957.

ADB975769 QPX Romford OHLM Depot. RM & EE OHLM Staff & Office Coach. Converted on lot 3955, 1978.
Formerly BR Mk1 BSK E35251, to dia 181 on lot 30427 Wolverton 1957.

ADB975770 QPX Romford OHLM Depot. RM & EE OHLM Staff & Office Coach. Converted on lot 3955, 1978.
Formerly BR Mk1 TSO E4671, to dia 93 on lot 30375 York 1957.

ADB975771 QPX Romford OHLM Depot. RM & EE OHLM Staff & Office Coach. Converted on lot 3955, 1978.
Formerly BR Mk1 SK M25302, to dia 146 on lot 30349 Wolverton 1957.

RDB975793 QXV RTC, Derby. Track Research Section Generator Van. Converted 1978.
Formerly LNER design CCT E1329E, to dia 6 on lot 1223 York 1950.

ADB975796 QXW (Cardiff Cathays C&W Shops). Emergency Staff Coach. Converted 1978.
Formerly BR Mk1 RFO W4, to dia 36 on lot 30012 1951.

The following vehicles are RCE Staff and Dormitory Coaches for Twin Jib Cranes or Ballast Cleaners (QPV) and were converted in 1978 from TK/SKs to dia 146 (147*). All are allocated to the Eastern Region.

No.	Ballast Cleaner/ Twin Jib Crane	Formerly	Build Details	
DB975797	DRT78105	E25132*	Lot 30155 Wolverton	1956
DB975798	DR76319	M25343	Lot 30349 Wolverton	1957
DB975799	DR76305	E24457	Lot 30088 Swindon	1954
DB975801	DR76204	E24274	Lot 30026 York	1951
DB975802	DR76105	E24796	Lot 30137 BRCW	1954
DB975803	DR76320	E24815	Lot 30137 BRCW	1954
DB975804	DR76318	E25696	Lot 30426 Wolverton	1957

DB975805 QPV ER. RCE Staff & Dormitory Coach for Single Line Gantries. Converted 1978.
Formerly BR Mk1 TK E24972, to dia 146 on lot 30154 Derby 1956.

DB975807 QXV SR. RCE Gauging Van. Converted on lot 3963, 1978 to replace DS22.
Formerly SR BY S683S, to dia 3092 on lot RSCO A974 Ashford/Eastleigh 1938.

ADB975808 QXA Strawberry Hill EMU Depot. RM & EE Test Coach 'Romeo'. Converted 1979.
Formerly BR Mk1 TTO S3834, to dia 93 on lot 30054 Eastleigh 1953.

ADB975809 QXA Strawberry Hill EMU Depot. RM & EE Test Coach 'Juliet'. Converted 1979.
Formerly BR Mk1 TTO S4025, to dia 93 on lot 30149 Swindon 1956.

TDB975810 QXV ScR. Carriage Cleaning Instruction Coach. Converted 1978.
Formerly BR Mk1 BTO SC9268, to dia 183 on lot 30170 Doncaster 1955.

TDB975811 QTW ZH - Carlisle. Stock Movement Brake Coach. Converted 1979.
Formerly BR Mk1 BTK SC34724, to dia 181 on lot 30156 Wolverton 1955.

ADB975812 QWX BR. APT Tests Coach. OOU. Converted 1979.
Formerly HST Prototype power car W43000 (originally W41001) on lot 30875 Derby 1972.

ADB975813 QWX ZE. APT Tests Coach. OOU. Converted 1979.
Formerly HST Prototype power car W43001 (originally W41002) on lot 30875 Derby 1972.

ADB975814 QXA RTC, Derby. M & EE Test Car 10. Converted 1981.
Formerly BR Mk1 TF M11000 (latterly W41000), to dia 70 on lot 30848 Derby 1972.

The following vehicles are seat trimming materials stores vans (QRV) converted in 1979 from GWR or GWR design Siphon Gs for use between ZD and ZL. The requirement for them has now ceased.

No.	*Location*	*Formerly*	*Dia.*	*Build Details*
CDB975832	ZL, OOU	W1025W	O62	Lot 1751 Swindon 1952
CDB975833	ZD, OOU	W1029W	O62	Lot 1751 Swindon 1952
CDB975834	ZL, OOU	W1043W	O62	Lot 1768 Swindon 1953
CDB975836	ZD, OOU	W1321W	O62	Lot 1721 Swindon 1949
CDB975837	ZL, OOU	W1339W	O62	Lot 1721 Swindon 1949
CDB975838	ZL, OOU	W2758W	M34	Lot 1589 Swindon 1937
CDB975839	ZL, OOU	W2930W	M34	Lot 1651 Swindon 1940
CDB975840	ZL, OOU	W2941W	O33	Lot 1664 Swindon 1945
CDB975841	ZL, OOU	W2943W	O33	Lot 1664 Swindon 1945
CDB975842	ZL, OOU	W2976W	O33	Lot 1664 Swindon 1945
CDB975843	ZL, OOU	W2994W	O33	Lot 1664 Swindon 1945

ADB975844 EZ5X CJ. RM & EE Test Coach, Unit (935) 057. OOU. Converted 1980.
Formerly BR DMSO ('PEP' stock) S64305, to dia 861 on lot 30818, 1971.

ADB975845 EZ5T Derby St. Marys. RM & EE Test Coach, Unit (935) 056. OOU. Converted 1979.
Formerly BR MSO ('PEP' stock) S62427, to dia 862 on lot 30819, 1971.

ADB975846 EZ5T Derby St. Marys. RM & EE Test Coach, Unit (935) 056. OOU. Converted 1979.
Formerly BR MSO ('PEP' stock) S62428, to dia 862 on lot 30819, 1971.

ADB975847 EZ5X Derby St. Marys. RM & EE Test Coach, Unit (935) 056. OOU. Converted 1979.
Formerly BR DMSO ('PEP' stock) S64302, to dia 861 on lot 30818, 1971.

ADB975848 EZ5X Derby St Marys. RM & EE Test Coach, Unit (935) 056. OOU. Converted 1979.
Formerly BR DMSO ('PEP' stock) S64303, to dia 861 on lot 30818, 1971.

ADB975849 EZ5T CJ. RM & EE Test Coach, Unit (935) 057. OOU. Converted 1980.
Formerly BR MSO ('PEP' stock) S62426 to dia 862 on lot 30819, 1971.

ADB975850 EZ5T CJ. RM & EE Test Coach, Unit (935) 057. OOU. Converted 1980.
Formerly BR MSO ('PEP' stock) S62429, to dia 862 on lot 30819, 1971.

ADB975851 EZ5X CJ. RM & EE Test Coach, Unit (935) 057. OOU. Converted 1980.
Formerly BR DMSO ('PEP' stock) S64304, to dia 861 on lot 30818, 1971.

The following vehicles are seat trimming materials stores vans (QRV) converted in 1979 from GWR design Siphon Gs for use between ZD and ZL. The requirement for them has now ceased:

No.	Location	Formerly	Dia.	Build Details
CDB975854	ZL, OOU	W1042W	O62	Lot 1768 Swindon 1953
CDB975855	ZL, OOU	W1038W	O62	Lot 1768 Swindon 1953
CDB975856	ZL, OOU	W1011W	O62	Lot 1751 Swindon 1952
CDB975857	ZL, OOU	W1327W	O62	Lot 1721 Swindon 1949

CDB975858 QSV ZD. Barrier Coach for Tanzanian Stock. OOU. Converted 1979.
Formerly BR Mk1 BCK M21033, to dia 171 on lot 30132 Metro-Cammell 1954.

CDB975861 QSV ZD. Barrier Coach for Tanzanian Stock. OOU. Converted 1979.
Formerly BR Mk1 BTO E9239, to dia 183 on lot 30170 Doncaster 1955.

DB975862 QPV RCE Staff Coach for Viaduct Inspection Unit DR82101. Converted on lot 3981, 1979.
Formerly BR Mk1 FO W3012, to dia 72 on lot 30008 BRCW 1954.

ADB975863 QSA Basingstoke. Barrier Coach for Class 508. Condemned. Converted on lot 3969, 1979.
Formerly BR Mk1 TTO S3842, to dia 93 on lot 30054 Eastleigh 1953.

ADB975864 QSA ZY - Strawberry Hill EMU Depot. Barrier Coach for Class 455. Converted on lot 3969, 1979.
Formerly BR Mk1 TTO S3849, to dia 93 on lot 30054 Eastleigh 1953.

ADB975865	QSA	Basingstoke. Barrier Coach for Class 508. Condemned. Converted on lot 3969, 1979. *Formerly BR Mk1 TTO S3835, to dia 93 on lot 30054 Eastleigh 1953.*
ADB975866	QSA	(Woking Yard). Barrier Coach for Class 508. Condemned. Converted on lot 3969, 1979. *Formerly BR Mk1 SK S25953, to dia 147 on lot 30686 Derby 1962.*
ADB975867	QSA	ZY - Strawberry Hill EMU Depot. Barrier Coach for Class 455. Converted on lot 3969, 1979. *Formerly BR Mk1 RSO S1006, to dia 56 on lot 30014 York 1951.*
ADB975871	QRV	Exmouth Junction C&W Shops. RM & EE Stores Van, 'ENPARTS'. Converted 1979. *Formerly GWR design SIPHON G W1033W, to dia O62 on lot 1768 Swindon 1953.*
ADB975872	QRV	(St. Blazey C&W Shops). RM & EE Stores Van, 'ENPARTS'. Converted 1979. *Formerly GWR design SIPHON G W1036W, to dia O62 on lot 1768 Swindon 1953.*
RDB975874	QWQ	RTC, Derby. Prototype Railbus 'LEV 1'. Built RTC/Leyland, Workington 1979.
ADB975875	QSA	Strawberry Hill EMU Depot. Barrier Coach for Class 455 stock. Converted on lot 3969, 1979. *Formerly BR Mk1 BTK S34643, to dia 182 on lot 30143 Charles Roberts 1954.*
ADB975876	QXX	Oxley C.S. RM & EE Instruction Coach. Converted on lot 3974, 1979. *Formerly Pullman kitchen first HAWK (schedule no. 314) built Metro-Cammell 1960. Later E314E.*
DB975881	QPV	York Up Yard condemned awaiting disposal. RCE Instruction Coach. Converted 1979. *Formerly LNER design (Thompson) buffet lounge car SC1705E to dia. 352 Doncaster 1948, built for Flying Scotsman service. Converted to RB in 1959.*
KDB975888	QPV	Whitemoor Yard, condemned awaiting disposal to Mayer Newman, Snailwell. S&T Dormitory Coach. *Formerly BR Mk1 SLEP M2810 to dia 10 on lot 30379 Doncaster 1958.*
ADB975889	QRV	Strawberry Hill EMU Depot. RM & EE Stores Van. Converted 1979. *Formerly SR design GUV S4602S, to dia 3182 on RSCO L3228 Lancing 1949.*
ADB975890	QRV	Strawberry Hill EMU Depot. RM & EE Stores Van. Converted 1979. *Formerly SR design GUV S4597S, to dia 3182 on RSCO L3228 Lancing 1949.*
TDB975894	QRV	Coton Hill Yard, Shrewsbury. Parcel Movements Van. OOU. Converted 1979. *Formerly SR design GUV S4599S, to dia 3182 on RSCO L3228 Lancing 1949.*
ADB975896	EZ5D	RE. RM & EE De-Icing Coach, Unit (930) 013. Converted on lot 3976, 1982. *Formerly 4-Sub DMBSO S11287S, to dia 119 on RSCO E3506 Eastleigh 1950.*
ADB975897	EZ5D	RE. RM & EE De-Icing Coach, Unit (930) 013. Converted on lot 3976, 1982. *Formerly 4-Sub DMBSO S11388S, to dia 119 on RSCO E3506 Eastleigh 1950.*

The following vehicles are cable drum carriers belonging to the RM & EE (QVX), except those with L prefixes which belong to the Electrification Section, BRB and are coded QYX.

Converted on lot 3972, 1979:

No.	*Location*	*Formerly*	*Type*	*Dia*	*Build Details*	
ADB975898	CE	E24691	TK	146	Lot 30058 Cravens	1953
ADB975899	CE	M3716	TTO	92	Lot 30017 Cravens	1952
ADB975900	CL	E4409	TTO	93	Lot 30219 Swindon	1957
ADB975901	CL	M3751	TTO	93	Lot 30043 Doncaster	1953
ADB975902	LG	E15847	CK	126	Lot 30221 Metro-Cammell	1956
ADB975903	LG	M25340	SK	146	Lot 30349 Wolverton	1957
ADB975904	SP	M24429	TK	146	Lot 30030 Derby	1953
ADB975905	SP	E25105	SK	147	Lot 30155 Wolverton	1956

ADB975906	Salop Sidings, Stafford	E25161	SK	147	Lot 30155	Wolverton	1956
ADB975907	Salop Sidings, Stafford	E15754	CK	126	Lot 30179	Metro-Cammell	1955
ADB975908	SI	E25094	SK	147	Lot 30155	Wolverton	1956
ADB975909	SI	E4308	TSO	93	Lot 30207	BRCW	1956
ADB975910	Rugby OHLM Depot	E15757	CK	126	Lot 30179	Metro-Cammell	1955
ADB975911	Rugby OHLM Depot	E34736	BTK	181	Lot 30156	Wolverton	1955
ADB975912	BY	E15840	CK	126	Lot 30221	Metro-Cammell	1956
ADB975913	BY	E25003	SK	146	Lot 30208	Derby	1956
ADB975914	WN	E4448	TSO	93	Lot 30226	BRCW	1956
ADB975915	WN	E24994	SK	146	Lot 30208	Derby	1956
LDB975916	(Ipswich)	E13190	FK	116	Lot 30217	Swindon	1957
LDB975917	Prescot Street, OHLM Depot, Wigan	E4636	TSO	93	Lot 30172	York	1956

Converted on lot 3973, 1979:

ADB975918	GW	E4225	TSO	93	Lot 30172	York	1956
ADB975919	GW	E15712	CK	126	Lot 30179	Metro-Cammell	1955
ADB975920	Carstairs OHLM Depot	E25025	SK	146	Lot 30208	Derby	1956

Converted on lot 3975, 1979:

ADB975921	HE	E3714	TTO	92	Lot 30017	Cravens	1952
ADB975922	HE	E25026	SK	146	Lot 30208	Derby	1956
ADB975923	Romford OHLM Depot	M25238	SK	147	Lot 30230	Metro-Cammell	1957
ADB975924	Romford OHLM Depot	E25069	SK	147	Lot 30155	Wolverton	1956
ADB975925	Romford OHLM Depot	M24849	TK	146	Lot 30153	Derby	1955
ADB975926	(ZN for repair)	E24990	SK	146	Lot 30208	Derby	1956
ADB975927	Romford OHLM Depot	M25196	SK	147	Lot 30230	Metro-Cammell	1957
ADB975928	Romford OHLM Depot	E15758	CK	126	Lot 30179	Metro-Cammell	1957
ADB975929	Romford OHLM Depot	E3830	TTO	93	Lot 30054	Eastleigh	1953
LDB975930	(Stowmarket)	E25205	SK	147	Lot 30230	Metro-Cammell	1957
LDB975931	(Ipswich)	E4541	TSO	93	Lot 30243	York	1956
LDB975932	RTC, Old Dalby Test Track	E13196	FK	116	Lot 30217	Swindon	1957
LDB975933	(Stowmarket)	E4591	TSO	93	Lot 30243	York	1956
LDB975934	Prescot Street OHLM Depot, Wigan	E3871	TTO	93	Lot 30080	York	1953

KDB975937 QRV Grantham. S&T Stores Van. Converted 1980 for ZF Test Train.
Formerly LMS PIII BG M31092M, to dia 2007 on lot 1261 Wolverton 1939.

ADB975941 QQV TI. BTU Tool Van. Converted 1980 for ZF Test Train.
Formerly LMS PIII BG M31275M, to dia 2007 on lot 1357 Wolverton 1941.

KDB975943 QRV Grantham. S&T Stores Van. Converted 1980 for ZF Test Train.
Formerly LMS PIII BG M31060M, to dia 2007 on lot 1261 Wolverton 1939.

ADB975946 QVX BE. RM & EE OHLM Cable Drum Carrier. Converted on lot 3987, 1980.
Formerly BR Mk1 SK M25243, to dia 147 on lot 30230 Metro-Cammell 1957.

ADB975947 QVX BE. RM & EE OHLM Cable Drum Carrier. Converted on lot 3987, 1980.
Formerly BR Mk1 TK E24948, to dia 146 on lot 30154 Derby 1956.

ADB975948 QXA ZD - GW. APT Test Coach 11 & Barrier Coach. Converted on lot 3994, 1981.
Formerly BR Mk1 RU E1963, to dia 23 on lot 30632 Swindon 1961.

ADB975949 QXA ZD - GW. APT Test Coach 12 & Barrier Coach. Converted on lot 3994, 1981.
Formerly BR Mk1 RU E1988, to dia 23 on lot 30632 Swindon 1961.

RDB975956 QXV RTC, Mickleover, Laboratory 7. Phoenix. Fire Tests Coach. Converted 1980.
Formerly BR Mk1 BSK M35061, to dia 181 on lot 30233 Gloucester 1956.

ADB975957 QXV Crewe Stationery Stores. Local Stores Movement Van. Converted 1980.
Formerly BR Fish Van E87948, to dia 800 on lot 30384 Faverdale 1959.

ADB975960 QQV CA. BTU Tool Van. Converted 1980. Previously IUO41468.
Formerly SR PMV S1323S, to dia 3103 on RSCO A1031 Ashford 1939.

ADB975961 QRV Ferme Park Carriage Sidings, Hornsey. RM & EE Stores Van. Converted 1980. Previously IU041312.
Formerly LNER design Fish Van E87249, to dia 800 on lot 30125 Faverdale 1954.

DB975962	QPV	WR. RCE Staff & Dormitory Van. Converted 1980. *Formerly SR PMV S2129S, to dia 3103 on RSCO L1191 Lancing 1942.*
RDB975964	QRV	ZD. Stores Coach. Converted 1980. *Formerly Lea Valley Suburban TS E59466, to dia 597 on lot 30463 Derby 1958.*
ADB975965	QRV	NL. RM & EE Stores Van. Converted 1980. *Formerly BR Fish Van M87675, to dia 800 on lot 30344 Faverdale 1960.*
TDB975966	QRV	Horsham, operates on every region. Chipmans' Weedkilling Train Stores Van. Converted 1980. *Formerly SR design GUV S4604S, to dia 3182 on RSCO L3228 Lancing 1949.*
TDB975967	QRV	Horsham, operates on every region. Chipmans' Weedkilling Train Stores Van. Converted 1980. *Formerly SR design GUV S4605S, to dia 3182 on RSCO L3228 Lancing 1949.*
ADB975968	QXV	RTC, Derby. M & EE Fire Tests Coach. Converted 1980. *Formerly BR Mk1 FK E13116, to dia 116 on lot 30107 Swindon 1954.*
ADB975969	QXV	Derby St. Marys. M & EE Fire Tests Coach. Converted 1980. *Formerly BR Mk1 FK E13189, to dia 116 on lot 30217 Wolverton 1957.*
ADB975970	QXV	Derby St. Marys. M & EE Fire Tests Coach. Converted 1980. *Formerly BR Mk1 FK E13200, to dia 116 on lot 30217 Swindon 1957.*

The following vehicles are class 313/315 barrier coaches (QSA), converted on lot 3998, 1980 from BR Mk1 RUOs to dia 61 on lot 30647 Wolverton 1961. They work between ZN and HE/IL.

No.	*Formerly*
ADB975971	E1054
ADB975972	E1039
ADB975973	E1021
ADB975974	E1030
ADB975975	E1042
ADB975976	E1033
ADB975977	E1023
ADB975978	E1025

ADB975980	QSA	WR. HST Barrier Coach. Converted 1980. *Formerly BR Mk1 RU W1967, to dia 23 on lot 30632 Swindon 1961.*
ADB975981	QSA	WR. HST Barrier Coach. Converted 1980. *Formerly BR Mk1 RU W1983, to dia 23 on lot 30632 Swindon 1961.*
ADB975982	QSA	WR. HST Barrier Coach. Converted 1980. *Formerly BR Mk1 RU W1987, to dia 23 on lot 30632 Swindon 1961.*
RDB975983	QXA	RTC, Derby. Stress Measurement Coach. Converted 1980. *Formerly BR Mk3a TSO M12162, to dia 111 on lot 30877 Derby 1975.*
RDB975984	QXA	RTC, Derby.Test Coach. Converted 1980. *Formerly BR Mk3 TRB M10000 (latterly W40000), to dia 42 on lot 30849 Derby 1973.*
ADB975985	QRV	RTC, Derby. M & EE Stores Coach. Converted 1980. *Formerly BR Mk1 BSO E9329, to dia 183 on lot 30443 Gloucester 1959.*

The following vehicles were converted in 1980 from LMS or LMS design period III BGs to form the ZC diesel locomotive test train (QXV):

No.	*Location*	*Formerly*	*Dia*	*Build Details*		
ADB975986	DY. OOU	M31359M	2171	Lot 1508	Wolverton	1950
ADB975987	DY. OOU	M30977M	2007	Lot 1096	Wolverton	1938
ADB975988	DY. OOU	M31057M	2007	Lot 1260	Derby	1940
ADB975989	DY. OOU	M31181M	2007	Lot 1305	Wolverton	1941
ADB975990	DY. OOU	M31254M	2007	Lot 1357	Wolverton	1941
ADB975991	Crewe South Yard, OOU	M31045M	2007	Lot 1260	Derby	1940
ADB975992	DY. OOU	M31904M	2100	Lot 1359	Wolverton	1944

RDB975993	QXV	Derby St. Marys. Fire Tests Coach. Converted 1980. *Formerly Lea Valley Suburban TS E59458, to dia 597 on lot 30463 Derby 1958.*

TDB975994	QWV	RTC, Derby. Test and Stores Car for Class 150 Stock. *Formerly Class 122 DMBS 55014, to dia 539 on lot 30419 Gloucester 1958.*
TDB975995	QRV	Wolverhampton. Stores Van. *Formerly LMS PIII BG M31257M, to dia 2007 on lot 1357 Wolverton 1941.*
ADB975997	QRV	(New Cross Gate C&W Shops). RM & EE Stores Van. Converted 1980. *Formerly SR design PMV S1562S, to dia 3103 on RSCO A3590 Ashford 1950.*
ADB975999	QSA	ZD. Barrier Coach for Mk3a Sleeping Cars. Converted 1981. *Formerly BR Mk1 FO E3054, to dia 73 on lot 30091 Doncaster 1954.*
DB977000	QPV	Perth Engineers' Yard. Scottish Highlands RCE Staff Coach. Converted 1981. *Formerly BR Mk1 RMB SC1844, to dia 98 on lot 30507 Wolverton 1960.*
DB977001	QXV	(Georgemas Jn). Scottish Highlands RCE Staff Training Coach. Converted 1981. *Formerly BR Mk1 RMB SC1843, to dia 98 on lot 30507 Wolverton 1960.*
ADB977006	QPV	(SG). Under conversion from a RCE Staff Coach to a BTU Coach. *Formerly BR Mk1 BSK E35277, to dia 181 on lot 30573 Gloucester 1960.*
ADB977008	QQV	AY. BTU Tool Van. Converted 1981. *Formerly BR Mk1 BG E81310, to dia 711 on lot 30323 Pressed Steel 1957.*
ADB977010	QQV	HG. BTU Tool Van. Converted 1981 to replace ADS6. *Formerly SR design CCT S2527S, to dia 3103 on RSCO L3764 Lancing 1955.*
DB977011	QVV	Ely. Pooley Weighing Machine Contractors' Staff & Tool Van. Converted 1981. *Formerly BR Mk1 CCT E94664, to dia 816 on lot 30564 Earlstown 1961.*
ADB977012	QQV	ED. BTU Tool Van. Converted 1981. *Formerly BR Mk1 BG M80957, to dia 711 on lot 30162 Pressed Steel 1957.*
DB977015	QRV	York Leeman Road Engineers' Yard. RCE Weedkilling Train Stores Van. Converted 1981. *Formerly BR Mk1 BG M81372, to dia 711 on lot 30400 Pressed Steel 1957.*
DB977016	QRV	York Leeman Road Engineers' Yard. RCE Weedkilling Train Stores Van. Converted 1981. *Formerly BR Mk1 BG M81304, to dia 711 on lot 30323 Pressed Steel 1957.*
DB977019	QPV	WR. RCE Staff & Dormitory Van for Twin Jib Crane DRP78215. Converted 1981, as Prototype. *Formerly BR Mk1 CCT S94393, to dia 816 on lot 30562 Earlestown 1960.*
CDB977021	QSV	ZD. Barrier Coach. Converted on lot 4020, 1981. *Formerly BR Mk1 BCK E21098, to dia 171 on lot 30185 Metro-Cammell 1956.*
CDB977022	QSV	ZD. Barrier Coach. Converted on lot 4020, 1981. *Formerly BR Mk1 BCK W21190, to dia 172 on lot 30424 Charles Roberts 1958.*

The following vehicles are stores vans based at Crewe Stationery Stores (QRV), and were converted in 1981 from LMS design PIII BGs to dia 2171. Their duties take them all over BR, except for XDB977029 which is condemned at ZN.

No.	*Formerly*	*Build Details*
XDB977023	M31420M	Lot 1588 Wolverton 1950
XDB977024	M31402M	Lot 1579 Derby 1950
XDB977025	M31393M	Lot 1563 Derby 1949
XDB977026	M31388M	Lot 1563 Derby 1949
XDB977027	M31409M	Lot 1579 Derby 1950
XDB977028	M31401M	Lot 1579 Derby 1950
XDB977029	M31403M	Lot 1579 Derby 1950
XDB977030	M31368M	Lot 1508 Wolverton 1949
XDB977031	M31361M	Lot 1508 Wolverton 1949
XDB977032	M31384M	Lot 1563 Derby 1949
XDB977033	M31351M	Lot 1508 Wolverton 1949
XDB977034	M31387M	Lot 1563 Derby 1949
XDB977035	M31385M	Lot 1508 Wolverton 1949

XDB977036	M31397M	Lot 1563 Derby	1949
XDB977037	M31407M	Lot 1579 Derby	1950

DB977038 QPW SR. RCE Staff & Tool Van. Converted 1981.
Formerly SR PMV S1728S, to dia 3103 on RSCO L1659 Lancing 1943.

TDB977040 QRV WB. Refuse Disposal Van. Converted 1981.
Formerly LMS PIII BG M31139M, to dia 2007 on lot 1304 Derby 1940.

TDB977041 QRV WB. Refuse Disposal Van. Converted 1981.
Formerly LMS PIII BG M31315M, to dia 2007 on lot 1357 Wolverton 1941.

TDB977042 QRV WB. Refuse Disposal Van. Converted 1981.
Formerly LMS PIII BG M31331M, to dia 2007 on lot 1444 Wolverton 1947.

TDB977043 QRV WB. Refuse Disposal Van. Converted 1981.
Formerly LMS PIII BG M31391M, to dia 2171 on lot 1563 Derby 1949.

ADB977044 QQV CR. BTU Tool Van. Converted 1981.
Formerly BR Mk1 CCT E94651, to dia 711 on lot 30564 Earlestown 1961.

ADB977045 QRV CP - Crewe Station. RM & EE Stores Van. Converted 1981.
Formerly SR design PMV S1629S, to dia 3103 on RSCO A3590 Ashford 1950.

The following were converted on lot 4019, 1981 from class 105 DTCLs (977047 - class 103) to 'Sandite' coaches (QXV):

No.	*Location*	*Formerly*	*Dia*	*Build Details*		
ADB977047	SP	M56156	645	Lot 30287	Park Royal	1957
ADB977048	BX	M56142	562	Lot 30282	Cravens	1957
ADB977049	BS	M56474	549	Lot 30504	Cravens	1959
ADB977050	CH	M56448	533	Lot 30470	Cravens	1958
ADB977051	(CW)	M56427	533	Lot 30470	Cravens	1958
ADB977052	TO	M56145	526	Lot 30285	Cravens	1957

The following vehicles form the ZF test train, QXV, and are based at Doncaster Freight Depot Sidings. They were converted in 1981 from BR Mk1s.

No.	*Formerly*	*Type*	*Dia*	*Build Details*		
ADB977053	M34526	BTK	181	Lot 30095	Wolverton	1955
ADB977054	M15997	CK	126	Lot 30351	Wolverton	1956
ADB977055	M15945	CK	126	Lot 30317	Wolverton	1956
ADB977056	M15989	CK	126	Lot 30351	Wolverton	1956
ADB977057	M24026	TK	146	Lot 30002	Derby	1951
ADB977058	M24428	TK	146	Lot 30030	Derby	1953
ADB977059	M24858	TK	146	Lot 30153	Derby	1955
ADB977060	M15994	CK	126	Lot 30351	Wolverton	1956
ADB977061	M15988	CK	126	Lot 30351	Wolverton	1956
ADB977062	W34545	BTK	181	Lot 30095	Wolverton	1955

ADB977063 QRX AF-ZG. RM & EE Stores Van. Converted 1981.
Formerly BR Mk1 CCT M94867, to dia 816 on lot 30614 Earlestown 1961.

ADB977064 QRV Ferme Park Carriage Sidings, Hornsey. RM & EE Stores Van. Converted 1981.
Formerly BR Fish Van E87894, to dia 800 on lot 30384 Faverdale 1959.

ADB977065 QRV Strawberry Hill EMU Depot. RM & EE Stores Van. Converted 1982.
Formerly SR B S232S, to dia 3093 on RSCO L1029 Lancing/Eastleigh 1939.

ADB977067 QRV Strawberry Hill EMU Depot. RM & EE Stores Van. Converted 1982.
Formerly SR B S382S, to dia 3093 on RSCO A927 Ashford/Eastleigh 1938.

ADB977068 EZ5Q SG. RM & EE Stores Unit (931) 019. Converted on lot 4022, 1983 to replace ADS70315.
Formerly 2-Hap DMBSO S14549S, to dia

ADB977069 EZ5Q SG. RM & EE Stores Unit (931) 019. Converted on lot 4022, 1983 to replace ADS70318.

The following are RCE Stores Vans (QRV) converted 1981 from BR Mk1 CCTs to dia 816:

No.	Location	Formerly	Build Details
DB977070	WR	M94107	Lot 30549 Earlestown 1959
DB977071	WR	S94336	Lot 30562 Earlestown 1960
DB977072	WR	W94502	Lot 30563 Earlestown 1960
DB977073	WR	W94518	Lot 30563 Earlestown 1960
DB977074	WR	E94635	Lot 30564 Earlestown 1961
DB977075	WR	E94662	Lot 30564 Earlestown 1961

ADB977076 QQX CF. BTU Tool Van. Converted 1981.
Formerly BR Mk1 CCT M94713, to dia 816 on lot 30614 Earlestown 1961.

ADB977077 QRV (New Cross Gate C&W Shops). RM & EE Stores Van. Converted 1982. Previously 083524.
Formerly SR B S396S, to dia 3093 on RSCO A927 Ashford/Eastleigh 1938.

DB977078 QPV (Crianlarich Upper). Glasgow North RCE Staff Coach. Converted 1982 to replace DB975584.
Formerly BR Mk1 RMB SC1817, to dia 99 on lot 30520 Wolverton 1960.

ADB977079 QRV Basingstoke. RM & EE Stores Van. Condemned. Converted 1981.
Formerly BR Mk1 CCT M94884, to dia 816 on lot 30614 Earlestown 1961.

ADB977080 QQV WY. BTU Tool Van. Converted 1981.
Formerly BR Mk1 CCT W94631, to dia 816 on lot 30564 Earlestown 1961.

ADB977081 QXA (RTC, Derby). ZC Test Train Coach. Converted 1982.
Formerly BR Mk1 FK M13267, to dia 116 on lot 30578 Metro-Cammell 1960.

ADB977082 QXA CE. ZC Test Train Coach. Converted 1982.
Formerly BR Mk1 RKB M1511, to dia 25 on lot 30514 Cravens 1959.

ADB977083 QXA CE. ZC Test Train Coach. Converted 1982.
Formerly BR Mk1 RKB M1552, to dia 25 on lot 30624 Cravens 1961.

ADB977084 QXA CE. ZC Test Train Coach. Converted 1982.
Formerly BR Mk1 RKB M1505, to dia 25 on lot 30514 Cravens 1959.

ADB977085 QXA CE. ZC Test Train Coach. Converted 1982.
Formerly BR Mk1 RF M336, to dia 17 on lot 30633 Swindon 1962. Converted 1970 to RBK M1637 to dia 26.

ADB977087 QSA Strawberry Hill EMU Depot. Barrier Coach for class 455 stock. Converted on lot 3969.
Formerly BR Mk1 BTK S34971, to dia 182 on lot 30229 Metro-Cammell 1956.

ADB977088 QQA WD. BTU Tool Van. Converted in 1985 at SG from a Barrier Coach.
Formerly BR Mk1 BTK S34990, to dia 182 on lot 30229 Metro-Cammell 1956.

RDB977089 QXA RTC, Derby. HST Executive Livery Demonstration Coach.
Formerly BR Mk1 TRK M10100 (latterly W40500), to dia on lot 30850 Derby 1973.

RDB977091 QXA RTC, Derby. BREL/Leyland Experimental Coach. Built at Leyland Workington 1982. Constructed on U/F BR Mk1 BCK E21234, to dia 171 on lot 30574 Gloucester 1960.

KDB977092 QTV (SG). S&T Brake Coach. OOU. Converted 1982.
Formerly BR Mk1 BCK SC21201, to dia 171 on lot 30425 Metro-Cammell 1958.

KDB977093 QTV Basingstoke. S&T Brake Coach. Condemned. Converted 1982.
Formerly BR Mk1 BCK SC21203, to dia 171 on lot 30425 Metro-Cammell 1958.

KDB977094 QTV Basingstoke. S&T Brake Coach. Condemned. Converted 1982.
Formerly BR Mk1 BCK SC21205, to dia 171 on lot 30425 Metro-Cammell 1958.

ADB977095 QTV (SG). Under conversion from a S&T Brake Coach to a BTU Coach.
Formerly BR Mk1 BCK SC21210, to dia 171 on lot 30425 Metro-Cammell 1958.

ADB977096 QQV SB. BTU Tool Van. Converted 1982 to replace ADB975418.
Formerly BR Mk1 BG M81549, to dia 711 on lot 30484 Pressed Steel 1958.

DB977097 QRV WR. RCE Stores Van. Converted 1982.
Formerly BR Mk1 CCT W94501, to dia 816 on lot 30563 Earlestown 1960.

DB977098 QPV (FW). Glasgow North RCE Staff Coach. Converted 1982 to replace DB975878.
Formerly BR Mk1 RMB SC1829, to dia 99 on lot 30520 Wolverton 1960.

ADB977099 QQV TE. BTU Tool Van. Converted 1982.
Formerly BR Mk1 BG E80833, to dia 711 on lot 30144 Cravens 1955.

CDB977100 QSV ZY - Strawberry Hill EMU Depot. Barrier Coach for Class 455. Converted 1982.
Formerly BR Mk1 SK M25623, to dia 146 on lot 30426 Wolverton 1957.

CDB977101 QSV ZY - Strawberry Hill EMU Depot. Barrier Coach for Class 455. Converted 1982.
Formerly BR Mk1 CK M15936, to dia 126 on lot 30317 Wolverton 1956.

CDB977102 QSV ZY - Strawberry Hill EMU Depot. Barrier Coach for Class 455. Converted 1982.
Formerly BR Mk1 SK E25236, to dia 147 on lot 30230 Metro-Cammell 1957.

CDB977103 QSV ZY - Strawberry Hill EMU Depot. Barrier Coach for Class 455. Converted 1982.
Formerly BR Mk1 TK M24899, to dia 146 on lot 30153 Derby 1955.

ADB977104 QRV Darnall C&W Depot. RM & EE Stores Van. Converted 1982.
Formerly BR Mk1 CCT M94911, to dia 816 on lot 30651 Earlestown 1961.

ADB977105 QRV Darnall C&W Depot. RM & EE Stores Van. Converted 1982.
Formerly BR Mk1 CCT M94763, to dia 816 on lot 30614 Earlestown 1961.

KDB977106 QTV Basingstoke. S&T Brake Coach. Condemned. Converted 1982.
Formerly BR Mk1 BCK SC21200, to dia 171 on lot 30425 Metro-Cammell 1958.

KDB977107 QTV (CJ) S&T Brake Coach. OOU. Converted 1982.
Formerly BR Mk1 BCK SC21202, to dia 171 on lot 30425 Metro-Cammell 1958.

KDB977108 QTV Basingstoke. S&T Brake Coach. Condemned. Converted 1982.
Formerly BR Mk1 BCK W21152 to dia 172 on lot 30187 Charles Roberts 1956.

ADB977109 QPA WD. BTU Staff Coach. Converted in 1985 at SG from a S&T Brake Coach.
Formerly BR Mk1 BCK S21271, to dia 172 on lot 30732 Derby 1964.

KDB977110 QTV (CJ). S&T Brake Coach. OOU. Converted 1982.
Formerly BR Mk1 BSK S34936, to dia 182 on lot 30229 Metro-Cammell 1956.

ADB977111 QRV New Cross Gate. BRUTE Repair Van. Converted 1982.
Formerly SR B S222S, to dia 3093 on RSCO L1029 Lancing/Eastleigh 1939.

ADB977112 QRV New Cross Gate. BRUTE Repair Van. Converted 1982.
Formerly SR B S248S, to dia 3093 on RSCO L1029 Lancing/Eastleigh 1939.

ADB977113 QRX SE - ZG. RM & EE Stores Van. Converted 1982.
Formerly BR Mk1 CCT M94772, to dia 816 on lot 30614 Earlestown 1961.

ADB977114 QXV CW. 'Sandite' Coach. Converted on lot 4027, 1982.
Formerly Class 105 DTCL M56129, to dia 526 on lot 30283 Cravens 1957.

ADB977115* EZ5V Kirkdale EMU Depot. 'Sandite' Coach, coupled to M28672M & M29271M. Converted on lot 4029, 1982.
Formerly LMS TC (latterly TS) M29702, to dia 2005 on lot 1012, 1938.

ADB977116 QRX SR. RM & EE Stores Van. Converted 1983.
Formerly BR Mk1 CCT M94212, to dia 816 on lot 30549 Earlestown 1959.

ADB977117 QRV BJ. RM & EE Stores Van. Converted 1982.
Formerly SR design PMV S1591S, to dia 3103 on RSCO A3490 Ashford/Lancing 1950.

KDB977118 QPV Exeter Red Cow Crossing. S&T Contractor's Staff & Tool Coach. Converted 1982.
Formerly BR Mk1 BTK W35024, to dia 182 on lot 30232 Gloucester 1956.

ADB977121 QRV WR. Wheel Wagon. Converted 1983.
Formerly BR Mk1 CCT M94868, to dia 816 on lot 30614 Earlestown 1961.

ADB977122 QPB Toton C&W Shops. BTU Staff Coach. OOU. Converted 1982.
Formerly BR Mk1 RB M1751, to dia 24 on lot 30527 BRCW 1961.

TDB977123 QWV LN. Route Learning Car, coupled to TDB977125.
Formerly Class 105 DMBS E51286, to dia 532 on lot 30469 Cravens 1958.

TDB977124 QWV LN. Route Learning Car, coupled to TDB977126.
Formerly Class 105 DMBS E51296, to dia 532 on lot 30469 Cravens 1958.

TDB977125 QWV LN. Route Learning Car, coupled to TDB977123.
Formerly Class 105 DTCL E56444, to dia 533 on lot 30470 Cravens 1958.

TDB977126 QWV LN. Route Learning Car, coupled to TDB977124.
Formerly Class 105 DTCL E56445, to dia 533 on lot 30470 Cravens 1958.

TDB977127 QXV MODAD Moreton-On-Lugg. Special Instruction Coach. Converted 1983.
Formerly BR Mk1 RB M1710, to dia 24 on lot 30512 BRCW 1960.

TDB977129 QXV MODAD Moreton-On-Lugg. Special Instruction Coach. Converted 1983.
Formerly BR Mk1 SK E25567 to dia 146 on lot 30426 Wolverton 1957.

TDB977132 QXV MODAD Moreton-On-Lugg. Special Instruction Coach. Converted 1983.
Formerly BR Mk1 FK E13231, to dia 116 on lot 30432 Swindon 1959.

ADB977133 QTX WB - DY. Stock Movement Brake Coach. Converted 1983.
Formerly BR Mk1 BTO M9226, to dia 183 on lot 30170 Doncaster 1955.

ADB977134 QTX WB - DY. Stock Movement Brake Coach. Converted 1983.
Formerly BR Mk1 BTO M9208, to dia 183 on lot 30170 Doncaster 1955.

ADB977135 QTX WB - DY. Stock Movement Brake Coach. Converted 1983.
Formerly BR Mk1 BTO M9225, to dia 183 on lot 30170 Doncaster 1955.

LDB977136 QYV (ZD for repair). Electrification Section Staff Coach. Converted 1983.
Formerly BR Mk1 BSK E35353, to dia 181 on lot 30699 Wolverton 1962.

ADB977137 QQV KD. BTU Tool Van. Converted 1983.
Formerly LMS design PIII BG M31367M, to dia 3171 on lot 1508 Wolverton 1949.

KDB977138 QRV (Stonebridge Park C&W Shops). S&T Stores Van. Converted 1983.
Formerly BR Mk1 CCT M94240, to dia 816 on lot 30549 Earlestown 1959.

KDB977139 QRV (Crewe S&T Yard). S&T Stores Van. Converted 1983.
Formerly BR Mk1 CCT M94300, to dia 816 on lot 30549 Earlestown 1959.

KDB977140 QRV (Bristol Kingsland Road). S&T Stores Van. Converted 1983.
Formerly BR Mk1 CCT M94429, to dia 816 on lot 30562 Earlestown 1960.

KDB977141 QRV (WB). S&T Stores Van. Converted 1983.
Formerly BR Mk1 CCT M94749, to dia 816 on lot 30614 Earlestown 1961.

KDB977142 QRV (Darnall S&T Yard). S&T Stores Van. Converted 1983.
Formerly BR Mk1 CCT M94824, to dia 816 on lot 30614 Earlestown 1961.

KDB977143 QPV Exeter Red Cow Crossing. S&T Staff & Tool Coach. Converted 1983.
Formerly BR Mk1 BTK W34944, to dia 182 on lot 30225 Charles Roberts 1956.

DB977144 QXA (LL). LMR RCE Track Recording Coach. Converted 1983 to replace DM395223.
Formerly BR Mk1 RBK M1622, to dia 46. Converted 1970 from BR Mk1 RF.

TDB977145 QXV (HT). Instruction Coach. Converted 1983.
Formerly BR Mk1 TSO E4721, to dia 93 on lot 30375 York 1957.

The following vehicles were converted from BR Mk1s in 1983 to form the ZC diesel locomotive test train (QXV) and all are based at Basford Hall Yard, Crewe:

No.	*Formerly*	*Type*	*Dia.*	*Build Details*	
ADB977146	E4841	TSO	89	Lot 30525 Wolverton	1959
ADB977147	M16123	CK	128	Lot 30666 Derby	1961
ADB977148	M16133	CK	128	Lot 30666 Derby	1961
ADB977149	M16137	CK	126	Lot 30577 Metro-Cammell	1960
ADB977150	E15642	CK	126	Lot 30158 Wolverton	1956
ADB977151	M25339	SK	146	Lot 30349 Wolverton	1957

DB977152 QQV WR. RCE Tool Van. Converted 1983.
Formerly BR Mk1 CCT M94250, to dia 816 on lot 30549 Earlestown 1959.

DB977153 QQV WR. RCE Tool Van. Converted 1983.
Formerly BR Mk1 CCT S94438, to dia 816 on lot 30562 Earlestown 1960.

DB977154 QQV WR. RCE Tool Van. Converted 1983.
Formerly BR Mk1 CCT M94226, to dia 816 on lot 30549 Earlestown 1959.

ADB977155 QQV ED. BTU Tool Van. Converted 1983.
Formerly BR Mk1 BG M80606, to dia 711 on lot 30046 York 1954.

The following vehicles were converted under lot 4038, 1984 at Slade Green to S&T Staff & Generator Coaches (QPW) for project 'MERCURY' from former BR Mk1 BTK/BSKs to diagram 181:

No.	*Location*	*Formerly*	*Build Details*
KDB977162	(Nottingham London Road)	SC35403	Lot 30700 Wolverton 1963
KDB977163	(Reading Goods)	E35487	Lot 30721 Wolverton 1963
KDB977164	(Great Bridge)	W34110	Lot 30025 Wolverton 1951
KDB977165	(Peterborough Spital)	E35408	Lot 30721 Wolverton 1963
KDB977166	(Worcester)	E35419	Lot 30721 Wolverton 1963
KDB977167	(Great Bridge)	E35400	Lot 30699 Wolverton 1963
KDB977168	(Biggleswade)	E35289	Lot 30573 Gloucester 1960

KDB977169 QPW Westbury. S&T Staff & Tool Coach. Converted 1983.
Formerly BR Mk1 BTK W35027, to dia 182 on lot 30232 Gloucester 1956.

ADB977170 QTV Darnall C&W Depot. Stock Movement Brake Coach. Converted 1983.
Formerly BR Mk1 BSK E35371, to dia 181 on lot 30699 1962.

RDB977171 QXA Leyland 'National' Bus Body Coach, not yet converted.
Formerly BR Mk1 TSO E4871, to dia 89 on lot 30525 Wolverton 1959.

ADB977172 QRV Gloucester/Worcester. RM & EE Stores and Workshop Coach. Converted 1983.
Formerly BR Mk1 BTK W35095, to dia 181 on lot 30233 Gloucester 1956.

TDB977173 QXV Crewe Gresty Lane. Train Crew Training Coach. Converted 1984.
Formerly BR Mk1 SK M25338 to dia 146 on lot 30349 Wolverton 1957.

TDB977174 QXV Crewe Gresty Lane. Train Crew Training Coach. Converted 1984.
Formerly BR Mk1 SK M25396, to dia 146 on lot 30349 Wolverton 1957.

TDB977175 QXV Crewe Gresty Lane. Train Crew Training Coach. Converted 1984.
Formerly BR Mk1 TSO M4440, to dia 93 on lot 30226 BRCW 1956.

TDB977176 QXV Crewe Gresty Lane. Train Crew Training Coach. Converted 1984.
Formerly BR Mk1 BSO E9300, to dia 183 on lot 30244 Doncaster 1956.

TDB977177 QWV ED. Driving Training/Route Learning/Sandite Car. Converted 1983.
Formerly Class 122 DMBS SC55015, to dia 539 on lot 30419 Gloucester 1958.

DB977178 QRV Toton RCE Yard. RCE Tunnel Inspection Stores Van. Converted 1984.
Formerly BR Mk1 CCT M94186, to dia 816 on lot 30549 Earlestown 1959.

DB977179 QRV Toton RCE Yard. RCE Tunnel Inspection Stores Van. Converted 1984.
Formerly BR Mk1 CCT M94190, to dia 816 on lot 30549 Earlestown 1959.

DB977180 QRV Toton RCE Yard, RCE Tunnel Inspection Stores Van. Converted 1984.
Formerly BR Mk1 CCT M94318, to dia 816 on lot 30561 Earlestown 1960.

DB977181 QRV Toton RCE Yard, RCE Tunnel Inspection Stores Van. Converted 1984.
Formerly BR Mk1 CCT M94700, to dia 816 on lot 30614 Earlestown 1961.

ADB977182 QR (ZL). RM & EE Stores Van. Converted 1983.
Formerly SR PMV S1507S, to dia 3103 on RSCO A3229 Ashford 1947.

ADB977183 QR (ZL). RM & EE Stores Van. Converted 1983.
Formerly SR PMV S1536S, to dia 3103 on RSCO A3229 Ashford 1947.

DB977184 QPV (FW). Glasgow North RCE Dormitory Coach. Converted 1984.
Formerly BR Mk1 SLF M2042, to dia 1 on lot 30377 York 1958.

DB977185 QPV (FW). Glasgow North RCE Dormitory Coach. Converted 1984.
Formerly BR Mk1 SLF W2010, to dia 1 on lot 30159 Wolverton 1958.

DB977186 QPV Muirhouse RCE Works. RCE Staff Coach. Converted 1984.
Formerly BR Mk1 RMB SC1835, to dia 99 on lot 30520, Wolverton 1960.

TDB977187 QXV Oxley CS. Train Crew Training Coach. Converted 1983.
Formerly BR Mk1 TK W24085, to dia 146 on lot 30002 Derby 1951.

TDB977188 QXV Oxley CS. Train Crew Training Coach. Converted 1983.
Formerly BR Mk1 TK W24430, to dia 146 on lot 30030 Derby 1953.

TDB977189 QXV Oxley CS. Train Crew Training Coach. Converted 1983.
Formerly BR Mk1 TK W24576, to dia 146 on lot 30057 BRCW 1953.

TDB977190 QXV Oxley CS. Train Crew Training Coach. Converted 1983.
Formerly BR Mk1 BSO E9341, to dia 183 on lot 30443 Gloucester 1959.

ADB977191	QXV	Basford Hall Yard, Crewe. ZC Diesel Locomotive Test Train. Converted 1983. *Formerly Class 100 DTCL M56106, to dia 537 on lot 30279 Gloucester 1957.*
DB977192	QSA	(ZL). For use with Track Testing Vehicles. Converted 1984. *Formerly BR Mk1 RUO E1067, originally FO M3145, to dia 73 on lot 30717 Swindon 1963 (renumbered and reclassified in 1976).*
DB977193	QSA	(ZL). For use Track Testing Vehicles. Converted 1984. *Formerly BR Mk1 RU W1989, to dia 23 on lot 30632 Ashford/Swindon 1961.*
TDB977194	QXV	MODAD Moreton-On-Lugg. Specal Instruction Coach. Converted 1983. *Formerly BR Mk1 TSO E4685, to dia 93 on lot 30375 York 1957.*
TDB977195	QXV	MODAD Moreton-On-Lugg. Special Instruction Coach. Converted 1983. *Formerly BR Mk1 SK E25171, to dia 147 on lot 30230 Metro-Cammell 1957.*
TDB977196	QXV	(Whitemoor Yard), condemned awaiting disposal to Mayer Newman, Snailwell. Special Instruction Coach. Converted 1983. *Formerly Class 100 DTCL M56111, to dia 532 on lot 30279 Gloucester 1957.*
TDB977197	QXV	MODAD Moreton-On-Lugg. Special Instruction Coach. Converted 1983. *Formerly BR Mk1 BSK E35346, to dia 181 on lot 30699 Wolverton 1962.*
ADB977199	QRV	(Exeter Red Cow Crossing). RM & EE Stores Van. Converted 1984. *Formerly LMS design PIII BG M31350M, to dia 2171 on lot 1508 Wovlerton 1949.*
DB977200	QQV	WR. RCE Tool Van for Rail Profiler DX 79105. Converted 1984. *Formerly BR Mk1 CCT W94444, to dia 816 on lot 30562 Earlestown 1960.*
DB977201	QQV	WR. RCE Tool Van. Converted 1984. *Formerly BR Mk1 CCT W94558, to dia 816 on lot 30563 Earlestown 1960.*
DB977202	QQV	Conversion not yet taken place. To be a WR RCE Tool Van. *Formerly BR Mk1 CCT W94676, to dia 816 on lot 30564 Earlestown 1961.*
DB977203	QQV	WR. RCE Tool Van. Converted 1984. *Formerly BR Mk1 CCT S94686, to dia 816 on lot 30564 Earlestown 1961.*
DB977204	QQV	Exeter Riverside Yard. RCE Tool Van. OOU. Converted 1984. *Formerly BR Mk1 CCT S94732, to dia 816 on lot 30614 Earlestown 1961.*
ADB977205	EZ5	Strawberry Hill. RM & EE Tractor Unit 051. Converted 1984. *Formerly BR 2-HAP DMBSO S61971, to dia 400 on lot 30711 Eastleigh 1963.*
ADB977206	EZ5	Strawberry Hill. RM & EE Tractor Unit 051. Converted 1984. *Formerly BR 2-HAP DTCL S76004, to dia 441 on lot 30712 Eastleigh 1963.*
ADB977207	EZ5X	Strawberry Hill. RM & EE Tractor Unit 054. Converted 1984. *Formerly BR 2-HAP DMBSO S61658, to dia 400 on lot 30617 Eastleigh 1961.*
ADB977208	EZ5	Strawberry Hill. RM & EE Tractor Unit 054. Converted 1984. *Formerly BR 2-HAP DTCL S75710, to dia 441 on lot 30618 Eastleigh 1961.*
ADB977209	EZ5X	Strawberry Hill. RM & EE Tractor Unit 052. Converted 1984. *Formerly BR 2-HAP DMBSO S61663, to dia 400 on lot 30617 Eastleigh 1961.*
ADB977210	EZ5	Strawberry Hill. RM & EE Tractor Unit 052. Converted 1984. *Formerly BR 2-HAP DTCL S75715, to dia 441 on lot 30618 Eastleigh 1961.*
ADB977211	EZ5X	Strawberry Hill. RM & EE Tractor Unit 053. Converted 1984. *Formerly BR 2-HAP DMBSO S61684, to dia 400 on lot 30617 Eastleigh 1961.*
ADB977212	EZ5	Strawberry Hill. RM & EE Tractor Unit 053. Converted 1984. *Formerly BR 2-HAP DTCL S75736, to dia 441 on lot 30618 Eastleigh 1961.*
ADB977213	EZ5X	Bl. RM & EE Temporary Stores Unit 020. Converted 1984. *Formerly BR4EPB DMBSO S61627, to dia 414 on lot 30582 Eastleigh 1961.*
ADB977214	EZ5	Bl. RM & EE Temporary Stores Unit 020. Converted 1984. *Formerly BR 2-HAP DTCL S75362, to dia 441 on lot 30453 Eastleigh 1959.*
ADB977215	QXV	WR. GWR 150 Exhibition Train Coach. Converted 1985. *Formerly BR Mk1 TSO E4323, to dia 93 on lot 30207 BRCW 1956.*
ADB977216	QXV	WR. GWR 150 Exhibition Train Coach. Converted 1985. *Formerly BR Mk1 TSO E4518, to dia 93 on lot 30243 York 1956.*
ADB977217	QXV	WR. GWR 150 Exhibition Train Coach. Converted 1984. *Formerly BR Mk1 TSO E4569, to dia 93 on lot 30243 York 1956.*
ADB977218	QXV	WR. GWR 150 Exhibition Train Coach. Converted 1985. *Formerly BR Mk1 TSO E4592, to dia 93 on lot 30243 York 1956.*

ADB977219	QXV	WR. GWR 150 Exhibition Train Coach. Converted 1985. *Formerly BR Mk1 BCK W21188, to dia 172 on lot 30424 Charles Roberts.*
ADB977220	QXV	Cardiff Cathays C&W Shos. GWR 150 Exhibition Train Stores Van. Converted 1984. *Formerly BR Mk1 BG M80578 to dia 711 on lot 30040 Wolverton 1954.*
ADB977221	QXV	WR. GWR 150 Exhibition Train Van. Converted 1984. *Formerly BR Mk1 BG M80854 to dia 711 on lot 30144 Craven 1955.*
DB977222	QRV	Chesterton Jn. Fisons Weedkilling Train Stores Van. Converted 1984. *Formerly BR Mk1 CCT M94869 to dia 816 on lot 30614 Earlestown 1961.*
TDB977223	QWV	HA. Driver Training/Route Learning/Sandite Car. Converted 1984. *Formerly Class 122 OMBS SC55007 to dia 539 on lot 30419 Gloucester 1958.*
DB977224	QQV	WR. RCE Tool Van. Converted 1984. *Formerly BR Mk1 CCT W94556 to dia 816 on lot 30563 Earlestown 1960.*
RDB977225	QWV	RTC, Derby. Laboratory Coach. Converted 1984. *Formerly Class 107 DMCL SC52014 to dia 649 on lot 30612 Derby 1961.*
RDB977226	QWV	RTC, Derby. Laboratory Coach. Converted 1984. *Formerly Class 107 TSL SC59787 to dia 647 on lot 30613 Derby 1961.*
RDB977227	QWV	RTC, Derby. Laboratory Coach. Converted 1984. *Formerly Class 107 DMCL SC52032 to dia 649 on lot 30612 Derby 1961.*
XDB977228	QRV	Conversion not yet taken place. To be a stores van based at Crewe Stationery Stores. *Formerly LMS design PIII BG M31390M to dia 2171 on lot 1563 Derby 1949.*
DB977229*	QVV	York Leeman Road. RCE Weedkilling Train Spray Van. Converted 1984. *Formerly BR Mk1 BG M80725 to dia 711 on lot 30140 BRCW 1955.*
ADB977230	QXV	WR. GWR 150 Exhibition Train Coach. Converted 1984. *Formerly BR Mk1 TSO E4298 to dia 93 on lot 30207 BRCW 1956.*
ADB977231	QXV	WR. GWR 150 Exhibition Train Coach. Converted 1984. *Formerly BR Mk1 TSO E4321 to dia 93 on lot 30207 BRCW 1956.*
ADB977232	QXV	WR. GWR 150 Exhibition Train Van. Converted 1984. *Formerly BR Mk1 CCT W94567 to dia 816 on lot 30563 Earlestown 1960.*
ADB977233	QXV	Conversion not yet taken place. To be an ER Instruction Coach. *Formerly BR Mk1 BSOT E9013, originally BSO E9368 to dia 184 on lot 30698 Wolverton 1963.*
ADB977234	QXV	Conversion not yet taken place. To be an ER Instruction Coach. *Formerly BR Mk1 TSO E4543 to dia 93 on lot 30243 York 1956.*
ADB977235	QQA	(CJ). BTU Tool Van. Converted 1984. Previously IU083172. *Formerly BR Mk1 BSK S34989 to dia 182 on lot 30229 MC 1956.*
TDB977236	QXV	MODAD Moreton-On-Lugg. Special Instruction Coach. Converted 1984. *Formerly BR Mk1 BSK W35134 to dia 182 on lot 30386 Gloucester 1957.*
TDB977237	QXV	?. To go to MODAD Moreton-On-Lugg as a Special Instruction Coach. Converted 1984. *Formerly BR Mk1 SK E25494 to dia 146 on lot 30374 York 1958.*
TDB977238	QXV	Conversion not yet taken place. To be a Special Instruction Coach. *Formerly BR Mk1 TSO E4232 to dia 93 on lot 30172 York 1956.*

The following numbers are allocated to RCE staff and dormitory vans (QPV) which are to be converted from BR Mk1 CCTs (dia 816). The prototype conversion is DB977019. No conversions have yet taken place:

No.	*Location*	*Formerly*	*Build Details*
DB977239			
DB977240			
DB977241			
DB977242			
DB977243			

DB977244	QQV	WR. RCE Tool Van. Converted 1984. *Formerly BR Mk1 CCT S94535 to dia 816 on lot 30563 Earlstown 1960.*
DB977245	QQV	WR. RCE Tool Van. Converted 1984. *Formerly BR Mk1 CCT S94748 to dia 816 on lot 30614 Earlestown 1961.*

ADB977246	QRV	LE. RM & EE Stores Van. Converted 1985. *Formerly BR Mk1 CCT W94526 to dia 816 on lot 30563 Earlestown 1960.*
TDB977247	QXV	Moreton in Marsh. Special Instruction Coach. Converted 1985. *Formerly BR Mk1 TK W24677 to dia 146 on lot 30058 Craven 1953.*
TDB977248	QXV	(York Up Yard). To go to Moreton in Marsh as a Special Instruction Coach. Converted 1985. *Formerly BR Mk1 TK E24679 to dia 146 on lot 30058 Craven 1953.*
DB977249	QPV	(Cardiff Cathays C&W Shops). RCE Staff Coach. Converted 1985. *Formerly BK Mk1 CK W7081 to dia 126 on lot 30471 MC 1959.*

The following numbers are allocated to RCE staff and dormitory vans (QPV) which are to be converted from BR Mk1 CCTs (dia 816). The prototype conversion is DB977019. No other conversions have yet taken place, although DB977250-60 have specific vehicles alloted to them:

No.	*Location*	*Formerly*	*Build Details*	
DB977250		W94538	Lot 30563 Earlestown	1960
DB977251		W94581	Lot 30563 Earlestown	1960
DB977252		M94291	Lot 30549 Earlestown	1960
DB977253		M94204	Lot 30549 Earlestown	1959
DB977254		M94241	Lot 30549 Earlestown	1959
DB977255		S94203	Lot 30549 Earlestown	1959
DB977256		S94261	Lot 30549 Earlestown	1959
DB977257		E94476	Lot 30563 Earlestown	1960
DB977258		M94436	Lot 30562 Earlestown	1960
DB977259		M94278	Lot 30549 Earlestown	1959
DB977260		W94570	Lot 30563 Earlestown	1960
DB977261				
DB977262				
DB977263				
DB977264				
DB977265				
DB977266				
DB977267				
DB977268				
DB977269				
DB977270				
DB977271				
DB977272				
DB977273				
DB977274				
DB977275				
DB977276				
DB977277				
DB977278				
DB977279				
DB977280				
DB977281				
DB977282				
DB977283				
DB977284				
DB977285				
DB977286				
DB977287				
DB977288				
DB977289				

ADB977290	EZ5Q	SR. RM & EE Stores Unit (931) 018. Converted 1985. *Formerly BR2-EPB DMBSO S65318 to dia 422 on lot 30116 Eastleigh 1955.*
ADB977291	EZ5Q	SR. RM & EE Stores Unit (931) 018. Converted 1985. *Formerly BR2-EPB DMBSO S65324 to dia 422 on lot 30116 Eastleigh 1955.*
ADB977292	QPV	ER. Asbestos Removal Staff Changing Room. Converted 1985. *Formerly BR Mk1 BTK E34059 to dia 181 on lot 30003 Derby 1951.*

This area intentionally blank for readers to add new conversions.

TDB 977334

RDB998900 ZWB RTC, Old Dalby Test Track. OHLM Inspection Car. OOU. Built by Drewry/Baguley in 1950 works number 2267.

RDB998901 ZWB RTC, Old Dalby Test Track. OHLM Inspection Card. Built by Drewry/Baguley in 1950 works number 2268.

The following LMR Inspection Saloons were constructed on lot 3093 1957 to LMS dia 2046 (RCE District Engineers' Saloon) under the 1957 Rolling Stock Programme.

DB999501 QXV Dock Street Siding, Preston.

DB999503 QXV Red Bank Carriage Sidings, Manchester.

DB999504 QXV DY.

RDB999507 QWV RTC, Derby. Self Propelled Laboratory. Built on lot 3248 Wickham 1958 as "Elliott" Track Recording Car.

The following WR Inspection Saloons were constructed on lot 3095, 1957 (TDB999506) and lot 3379, 1860 (DB999508/9) to WR dia Q13 (RCE District Engineers' Saloon) under the 1958/9 Rolling Stock Programmes.

TDB999506 QXV OM. WR General Manager.

DB999508 QXV Taunton Engineers' Yard. RCE Exeter Division.

DB999509 QXV Newport Godfrey Street. RCE Newport/Swansea Divisions.

DB999550 QXB RTC, Derby. High Speed Track Recording Coach. *This vehicle which was constructed on lot 30830 Derby 1976 was the last BR Mk2F vehicle to be built.*

DB975017, a welding demonstration coach is seen at Swindon on 19th May 1979. This vehicle was formerly a BR Mk1 brake third W9207. [Keith Gunner

DB999509, a purpose built inspection saloon of BR Mk1 design is seen parked in a siding near to Newport station. [C. J. Tuffs

DE NUMBER SERIES

The current fleet of DE vehicles started with DE320000 in 1950 and continued until DE321146 in 1971. However the implementation of TOPS meant that DE 321147 was allocated in 1973 to give a separate number to a TRM (track relaying machine) compressor wagon, while in 1974 DE321148 was allocated to eliminate a duplicate number. The surviving DE32xxxx vehicles are detailed below and include Thompson design coaches DE32113/4/31/4. Particularly worthy of mention is the fact that there are survivors from the North British Railway, the Great Northern Railway, the Great Central Railway and the Great Eastern Railway. The most active coach in this category is DE320444 built as long as as 1907! The majority of the survivors are LNER coaches. The LNER numbering system was most complex and for a full explanation the reader should consult "Gresley's Coaches" by Michael Harris. Originally new LNER coaches were allocated numbers from 10000 upwards, but in April 1925 a new system was introduced whereby the first number of the vehicle indicated the section to which the coach was allocated, i.e. 1 - East Coast Joint Stock, 2 - N.E., 3 - N.B., 4 - G.N., 5 - G.C., 6 - G.E., 7 - GNoS. This applied to both pre-grouping and LNER stock and numbers were allocated indiscriminately. When a coach was transferred from one section to another it was given a new number which bore no relationship to its former number. In 1946 most standard postgrouping vehicles were numbered in classes, taking for each class each section's vehicles in the order above, except that ECJS vehicles were not renumbered. Some GE section vehicles in the 6xxxx series were also not numbered.

Also detailed in this section and grouped together for convenience are the conversions from LNER design Fish Vans and BR Fish Vans.

The following are former LNER Fish Vans, to dia 214 built 1950:

ADE75205	ZRV	CR. RM & EE Stores Van. Converted 1977.
ADE75415	ZSV	HT. Steam Heating Boiler Van.

The following vehicles were formerly BR Fish Vans to dia 800 built at Faverdale. They were transferred to freight stock without being renumbered, and when passing into departmental service retained their original number with the addition of the departmental prefix, as is the practice for freight vehicles.

Lot 30125, 1954.

ADE87293	ZQV	NC. BTU Tool Van.
ADE87380	ZQV	TI. BTU Tool Van.

Lot 30344, 1960.

ADW87671	ZQV	WN. RM & EE OHLM Tool Van.
DW87674	ZQV	LMR. RCE Tool Van for Ballast Cleaner DR76219.

Lot 30384, 1959.

DW87771	ZQV	Kilmarnock RCE Workshops. RCE Tool Van.
ADW87795	ZQV	Rugby OHLM Depot. RM & EE OHLM Tool Van.

Lot 30442, 1961.

ADW87973	ZQV	(Temple Mills Yard). BTU Tool Van.
XDE 88043	ZRW	Crewe Stationery Stores. Local Stores Movement Van.
ADE321054	QQV	CA. BTU Tool Van. Converted 1954 to replace DE961520 at CR. Formerly TK E42440E.
ADE320388	QQV	SL. BTU Tool Van. Converted 1956. *Formerly LNER T E82445E, to dia 205 Gloucester 1935 (originally 64075 - built as composite).*
ADE320392	QQV	CA. BTU Tool Van. Converted 1956. At TE until 1957. *Formerly LNER T E82449E, to dia 205 Gloucester 1935 (originally 64079 - built as composite).*
DE320444	QPV	ER. RCE Staff & Dormitory Coach for Twin Jib Crane DRP78218. Converted 1957. *Formerly ECJS TK E52055E, to dia 22 Doncaster 1907 (originally 377 then 1377. Became 52055 in 1929).*
LDE320542	QYV	(ZD for repair). Electrification Section Workshop Coach. Converted 1957. *Formerly NBR TK SC3586E, built 1921 as NBR 586.*
ADE320580	QQV	Romford OHLM Depot. RM & EE OHLM Tool Van. Converted 1958. *Formerly LNER BT E86827E, to dia 202 Pickering & Co. 1935 (originally 62089).*

ADE320582 QXV Carstairs OHLM Depot. RM & EE OHLM Workshop Coach. Converted 1958.
Formerly LNER T E82399E, to dia 203 Pickering & Co. 1936 (originally 60097).

ADE320584 QXV Carstairs OHLM Depot. RM & EE OHLM Workshop Coach. Converted 1958.
Formerly LNER T E82395E, dia 203 Pickering & Co. 1936 (originally 60093).

ADE320610 QQV Tinsley Yard, condemned awaiting disposal to Passmore Edwards Museum, London. BTU Tool Van. Converted 1958.
Formerly GER BTK E62482E, to dia 547 built Mid C&W Co 1920 as GER 1019.

ADE320636 QQV NC. BTU Tool Van. Converted 1958 under 1955 programme.
Formerly GER BTK E62490E, to dia 547 built Mid C&W Co 1920 as GER 1027.

DE320644 QPV ER. RCE Staff & Dormitory Coach for Ballast Cleaner DR76312. Converted 1958.
Formerly LNER BTK E16130E, to dia 39 York 1926 (originally 5741).

DE320645 QPV York Leeman Road Engineers' Yard. RCE Staff & Dormitory Coach. Converted 1958.
Formerly LNER BTK E16847E, to dia 324 converted from BCK to dia 34 built York 1926 (originally 1083 then 24680).

ADE320659† QSV Romford OHLM Depot. Runner for Crane ADRT96308. Converted 1958.
Formerly GNR BCK E4252E built Doncaster 1912.

ADE320667 QSV Beighton Engineers' Yard. Runner for Crane ADRT96307. Converted 1962.
Formerly LNER BTK E16352E, to dia 114 York 1930 (originally 4942).

ADE320682 QSV (ZE for Repair). Runner for Crane ADRT96309. Converted 1958.
Formerly LNER locker composite E18047E to dia 8 Doncaster 1926 (originally 186).

ADE320692 QQV Perth Station Sidings. BTU Tool Van. Converted 1959.
Formerly LNER BTK E16175E, to dia 40 Doncaster 1926 (originally 62540).

ADE320721 QQV (ZH for Repair). BTU Tool Van. Converted 1959.
Formerly LNER BCK SC32361E, NER dia 256B, York 1924.

ADE320728 QPV HA. BTU Staff & Tool Coach. Converted 1959.
Formerly LNER TO SC12130E, to dia 27 Dukinfield 1927 (originally 22315).

ADE320740 QPV TE, condemned awaiting disposal to Cooper Metals, Sheffield. BTU Staff & Tool Coach. Converted 1959 under 1957 BTU programme.
Formerly LNER CK E18008E to dia 6 York 1926 (originally 63792).

KDE320759 QPV Ipswich Goods Yard. S&T Staff & Tool Coach. Converted 1959 to replace DE960923.
Formerly LNER BT E86072E, to dia 65 York 1926 (originally 3107).

DE320766 QSV Dinsdale Rail Welding Depot. Runner for Crane DRF81310. Converted 1959.
Formerly LNER BTK E62507E, NER dia 209 York 1924.

DE320767 QSV Dinsdale Rail Welding Depot. Runner for Crane DRF81311. Converted 1959.
Formerly LNER BTK E62508E, NER dia 209 York 1924.

DE320781 QXO Darnall C&W Depot. RCE Tunnel Inspection Coach. Cannabalised. Converted 1959.
Formerly NER BZ E2144E, to dia 1918.

ADE320797 QPV BH. BTU Staff & Tool Coach. Converted 1960.
Formerly LNER BTK E11047E, to dia 136 York 1928 (originally 4163).

DE320803 QPV (Lowestoft). RCE Staff & Tool Coach. Converted 1960.
Formerly LNER T E82347E, to dia 57 Gloucester 1927 (originally 61684).

DE320818 QSV Low Fell Engineers' Yard. Runner for Crane DRT80122. Converted 1960 for Crane DRG80109.
Formerly LNER F E81025E, to dia 48 York 1927 (originally 31875).

DE320821 QSV Perth Engineers' Yard. Runner for Crane DRT81318. Converted 1960.
Formerly LNER BT E86138E, to dia 65 York 1927 (originally 62575).

ADE320823 QPV Rugby North Sidings. RM & EE OHLM Staff & Office Coach. OOU. Converted 1960.
Formerly LNER CL E88014E, to dia 49 Midland RCW Co 1926 (originally 63788).

ADE320825	QXV	(ZD for Repair). RM & EE OHLM Workshop & Generator Van. Converted 1960. *Formerly LNER CL E88055E, to dia 50 York 1929 (originally 32508).*
ADE320828	QXV	Rugby North Sidings. RM & EE OHLM Workshop Coach. OOU. Converted 1960. *Formerly LNER C E88101E, to dia 51 Dukinfield 1928 (originally 32277).*
ADE320836	QXV	Rugby North Sidings. RM & EE OHLM Pantogrpah Coach. OOU. Converted 1960. *Formerly LNER T E82359E, to dia 57 York 1929 (originally 61696).*
DE320852	QSP	Low Fell Engineers' Yard. Runner for Crane DRT80123. Converted 1960 for Crane DRT80123. *Formerly LNER CL E88032E, to dia 50 Dukinfield 1929 (originally 32485).*
DE320853	QSV	Low Fell Engineers' Yard. Runner for Crane DRF81313. Converted 1960. *Formerly NER BZ E2161E. Built 1919 to dia 171.*
DE320854	QSV	Low Fell Engineers' Yard. Runner for Crane DRF81312. Converted 1960. *Formerly NER BZ E2164E. Built 1919 to dia 171.*
DE320855	QSV	Low Fell Engineers' Yard. Runner for Crane DRF81314. Converted 1960. *Formerly NER BZ E2192E. Built 1919 to dia 171.*
ADE320862	QQV	DR. BTU Tool Van. Converted 1961. *Formerly LNER SLF E1149E, to dia 17 Doncaster 1925 (10195 pre 1925).*
ADE320864	QQV	CR. BTU Tool Van. Converted 1960. *Formerly ECJS SLF E1174E, dia 64B York 1923.*
ADE320875	QXV	Stratford Market. RM & EE OHLM Office Coach. Converted 1960. *Formerly LNER CK E18032E, to dia 7 York 1924. Built for Flying Scotsman service. (Originally 1064 then 7766).*
DE320879	QSW	Norwich Engineers' Yard. Runner for Crane DRT81144. Converted 1961. *Formerly DE320407 (originally GNR goods brake van 449 built 1910).*
DE320881	QSW	Doncaster Engineers' Yard. Runner for Crane DRT81123. Converted 1961. *Formerly LNER BT E86159E, to dia 66 BRCW 1926 (originally 3647).*
DE320887	QSV	Dinsdale Rail Welding Depot. Runner for Crane DRF81309. Converted 1961. *Formerly LNER T E82116E, to dia 56 Metro CW 1926 (originally 22450, later 3854).*
DE320888	QPV	ER. RCE Staff and Dormitory Coach for Ballast Cleaner DR76311. Converted 1960 for viaduct inspection unit. *Formerly LNER SLF E1237E, to dia 17 Doncaster 1924 (10197 pre 1925).*
DE320893	QPV	ER. RCE Staff and Dormitory Coach for Twin Jib Crane DRC78231. Converted 1961. *Formerly LNER BTK E16065E, to dia 37A Doncaster 1929 (originally 41347).*
DE320894	QPV	Lowestoft. RCE Staff & Dormitory Coach. OOU. Converted 1961. *Formerly LNER TK E12466E, to dia 115 Metro-Cammell 1931 (originally 3374).*
KDE320899	QPV	Finsbury Park, condemned awaiting disposal to Bird, Long Marston. S&T Staff & Tool Coach. Converted 1961. *Formerly LNER CK E18028E, to dia 7 York 1925. Built for Flying Scotsman (originally 1062 then 64133).*
DE320907	QPV	ER. RCE Staff & Dormitory Coach for Ballast Cleaner DR76203. Converted 1961. *Formerly LNER RF E9019E, to dia 10C Doncaster 1929 (originally 1222 then 651).*
ADE320912	QPV	DR. BTU Staff & Tool Coach. Converted 1961 for LN. *Formerly LNER RF E9102E, to dia 10C Doncaster 1929 (originally 51773).*
ADE320921	QPV	GD. BTU Staff & Tool Coach. Converted 1961. *Formerly LNER TK E61703E, to dia 141 Metro CW 1930.*
DE320946	QPV	ER. RCE Staff & Dormitory Coach for Twin Jib Crane DRC78235. Converted 1962 for NER weedkilling train. *Formerly LNER TK E12961E, to dia 155 York 1936 (originally 3849).*
ADE320947	QPV	SF. BTU Staff & Tool Coach. Converted 1963. *Formerly LNER RF E9007E, to dia 10C Doncaster 1929 (originally 42969).*

DE320963	QSO	York Works. Runner for Crane RD15. Converted 1962. *Formerly LNER 32' four-wheeled milk van E70134E, to dia 87 Stratford 1927 (originally 6286).*
ADE320964	QSV	Lincoln. Runner for Crane ADRF96407. Converted 1962. *Formerly LNER 32' four-wheeled milk van E70135E to dia 87 Stratford 1927 (originally 6287).*
DE320966	QPV	ER. RCE Staff & Dormitory Coach for Twin Jib Crane DRS78202. Converted 1963. *Formerly LNER TK E12735E, to dia 115 York 1934 (originally 1459).*
DE320995	QVV	Lowestoft. RCE Weedkilling Train Spray Coach. OOU. Converted 1963. *Formerly LNER BTO E16551E, to dia 191 York 1935 (originally 43571).*
TDE320996	QSV	Beighton Engineers' Yard. Runner for Crane TDRF96406. Converted 1963. *Formerly LNER 32' four-wheeled generator van E70125E to dia 96 Stratford 1927 (originally 6277).*
ADE320997	QSV	GD. Runner for Crane ADRF96405. Converted 1963. *Formerly LNER BY E70228E, to dia 120 Stratford 1929 (originally 6836).*
ADE321012	ZZV	FW. Snowplough (tender mounted large plough). *Formerly LNER Loco Tender 5593.*
DE321015	QPV	Tinsley Yard, condemned awaiting disposal to South Yorks RPS. RCE Staff & Tool Van. *Formerly LNER CL E88026E, to dia 50 Dukinfield 1930 (originally 32455).*
DE321020	QPV	Perth Engineers' Yard. RCE Staff & Dormitory Coach. OOU. Converted 1964. 'NE Div 4'. *Formerly LNER RC SC9161E, to dia 187 Doncaster 1936 (originally 32567).*
ADE321047	QXV	Barking. ODM Generator Coach. Converted 1964. *Formerly BR Mk1 RFO E3, to dia 36 lot no. 30012 York 1951.*
DE321048	QPV	ER. RCE Staff & Dormitory Coach for Twin Jib Crane DRP78214. Converted 1964. *Formerly LNER TTO E60505E, to dia 216 York 1936.*
DE321049	QPV	ER. RCE Staff & Dormitory Coach for Viaduct Inspection Unit DR82002. Converted 1964. *Formerly LNER TTO E60525E, to dia 216 York 1936.*
DE321051	QSV	York Concrete Yard. Runner for Crane DRS81140. Converted 1964. *Formerly LNER 32' four-wheeled generator van E70130E, dia 86 Stratford 1926 (originally 6282).*
ADE321052	QPV	SF. BTU Tool Van. Converted 1965. *Formerly BR Mk1 BS M43240, to dia 371 lot no. 30047 Doncaster 1954.*
DE321055	QPV	Perth Engineers' Yard. RCE Staff & Dormitory Coach. OOU. Converted 1966. 'NE Div 7'. *Formerly LNER CK Sc18406E, to dia 296 Doncaster 1939 (originally 32431).*
DE321056	QPV	Perth Engineers' Yard. RCE Staff & Dormitory Coach. Converted 1966. 'NE Div 8'. *Formerly LNER CK E18246E, to dia 130 York 1938 (originally 24384).*
DE321057	QPV	Perth Engineers' Yard. RCE Staff & Dormitory Coach. OOU. Converted 1966. 'NE Div 9'. *Formerly LNER locker composite E18395E, to dia 251 Doncaster 1938. Built for Flying Scotsman service (originally 1854).*
ADE321061	QXV	Romford OHLM Depot. RM & EE OHLM Workshop Coach. Converted 1965. *Formerly LNER TO E12204E, to dia 27C Cravens 1936 (originally 22250).*
ADE321062	QXV	(ZD for repair). RM & EE OHLM Office Coach. Converted 1965. *Formerly LNER BTO E16548E, to dia 191 York 1935 (originally 43568).*
ADE321063	QQV	Romford OHLM Depot. RM & EE OHLM Tool Van. Converted 1965. *Formerly LNER TO E60548E, to dia 216 York 1935.*
ADE321064	QXV	Romford OHLM Depot. RM & EE OHLM Workshop Coach. Converted 1965. *Formerly LNER TTO E13494E, to dia 186 Metro-Cammell 1938 (originally 52254).*
TDE321069	QPV	Perth Station Sidings. Staff Changing Coach. Converted 1965. *Formerly LNER RB E9116E, to dia 167 York 1936 (originally 24080).*

TDE321070 QPV Perth Station Sidings. Staff Changing Coach. Converted 1965.
Formerly LNER TTO SC13279E, to dia 186 BRCW 1936 (originally 23981).

The following are steam heating boiler vans (ZSP) constructed in 1966 on former LNER plate wagon underframes.

No.	*Location*	*Former Wagon U/F*
ADE321071	CA	E251320
ADE321072	CA	E251077
ADE321073	KL	E250919
ADE321074	MR	E251092
ADE321075	HT	E251219
ADE321076	MR	E250537
ADE321077	GD	E251378
ADE321078	MR	E251200

ADE321088 QQV HM. BTU Tool Van. Converted 1965.
Formerly BK Mk1 BS M43344, to dia 371 30087 York 1955.

TDE321101 QXV GD. Steam Heating Boiler Van. Converted 1966.
Formerly BR Mk1 Horse Box E96347, to dia 751 on lot 30146 Earlstown 1957.

DE321107 QPV York Leeman Road Engineers' Yard. RCE Staff Van for Tunnel Gauging Vehicle DE230918. Converted 1966.
Formerly BR Mk1 Horse Box E96305, to dia 751 on lot 30146 Earlestown 1957.

ADE321109 QQV IS. BTU Tool Van. Converted 1966.
Formerly LNER BG E70170E, to dia 113 Dukinfield 1934 (originally 4028).

ADE321113 QYV (ZD for repair). RM & EE OHLM Staff & Office Coach. Converted 1967.
Formerly LNER TTO E13799E, to dia 330 York 1947.

ADE321114 QXY (ZD for repair). RM & EE Staff & Office Coach. Converted 1967.
Formerly LNER design TK E1570E to dia 329 York 1949.

ADE321131 QYV Wigan Bamfurlong. RM & EE OHLM Office Coach. OOU. Converted 1968.
Formerly LNER design TK M13863E to dia 329 York 1949.

DE321134 QPV York Leeman Road Engineers' Yard. RCE Staff & Dormitory Coach. Converted 1969.
Formerly LNER design BTK M13868E to dia 346 Doncaster 1949.

ADE321138 QXV (ZD for repair). RM & EE OHLM Pantograph Coach. Converted 1969.
Formerly LNER design TK E1556E to dia 329 York 1948.

ADE321139 QXV Romford OHLM Depot. RM & EE OHLM Pantograph Coach. Converted 1969.
Formerly LNER design TK E13817E to dia 329 BRCW 1948.

"Watford FC are magic" reads the inscription on the side of this ex-LNWR BG which was originally built as a world war 1 ambulance coach. This vehicle, now numbered TDM395455 is used as an operating department instruction coach at Watford Junction. [Mike Robinson

Ex LMS BG XDB977032, now a stores van based at Crewe, seen at Bristol Temple Meads on 21st October 1983. [Mike Ware

DM NUMBER SERIES

The current fleet of DM vehicles started with DM395001 in 1951 and continued until DM396007 in 1971. However the implementation of TOPS meant that in 1973/4 DM396008-11 were allocated to give individual numbers to a crane runner, a former internal user coach and two TRM compressor wagons. The oldest survivor is six wheeler DM395092 a passenger brake van built for the Midland Railway in 1913.

Most vehicles in this series are ex LMS coaches and are referred to as period I, II or III (PI, PII, PIII) according to the Essery and Jenkinson's descriptions.

Also grouped here are the last of the ADM40xxx stores vans, the ADM444xx steam heating boiler vans and the DM45xxx saloons.

L.M.S. DESIGN SIX-WHEELED FISH VANS TO DIA. 2115.
These vehicles were converted to stores vans (ENPARTS) with the addition of the AD prefix to their original numbers.

Lot 1509 Wolverton 1949.

ADM40320 Stonebridge Park C&W Shops, awaiting disposal to the GWR Preservation Group.
ADM40321 Bescot Yard. OOU.

The following former LMS PI TOs to dia 1745 on lot 185 Metro-Cammell 1926 were converted to Steam Heating Boiler Vans in 1960.

ADM44401	AC	*Formerly M8026M*
ADM44402	PC	*Formerly M8071M*
ADM44404	NH	*Formerly M8000M*
ADM44405	AC	*Formerly M8012M*
ADM44406	CL	*Formerly M8003M*
ADM44408	LG	*Formerly M8044M*
ADM44414	LL	*Formerly M8023M*
DM45020	QXV	EC. ScR General Managers Inspection Saloon. *Built to LMS, dia 2046 on lot 1356 Wolverton 1944.*
DM45026	QXV	Walsall Engineers' Yard. RCE Birmingham Division Inspection Saloon. *Built to LMS, dia 2046 on lot 1356 Wolverton 1944.*
DM45028	QXV	EC. ScR RCE Inspection Saloon. Replaced DW80969 in 1971. *Built to LMS, dia 2046 on lot 1327 Wolverton 1942.*
DM45029	QXV	Crewe Cresty Road. RCE Crewe Division Inspection Saloon. *Built to LMS, dia 2046 on lot 1327 Wolverton 1942.*
DM45030	QXV	EC. ScR RCE Inspection Saloon. Replaced DM45036 & DE320577. *Built to LMS, dia 2046 on lot 1327 Wolverton 1942.*
ADM45036	QPV	AY. BTU Staff Coach. *Built to LMS, dia 2046 on lot 1432 Wolverton 1947.*
DM45045	QXV	(ZH for repair). Inspection Saloon. *Built to LMS, dia 2046 on lot 1221 Wolverton 1940.*
TDM45047	QXV	MODAD Moreton-On-Lugg. Observation Saloon. Formerly Liverpool Division Engineers' Saloon. *Built to LMS, dia 2046 on lot 1264 Wolverton 1941.*
DM395092	QPV	Guide Bridge Engineers' Yard. RCE Staff & Dormitory Van for Crane DRT81264. Converted 1954 for LMR Weedkilling Train. *Formerly Midland (Bain) 6w BZ M34148M, to dia 530A on lot 788 Derby 1913.*
ADM395205	QPV	CD. BTU Staff & Tool Coach. Converted 1957. *Formerly LMS PI RFO (semi-open) M1023M, to dia 1707 on lot 379 Derby 1928.*
ADM395207	QPV	FW. BTU Staff & Tool Coach. Converted 1958. *Formerly LMS PI RFO (semi-open) M1026M, to dia 1707 on lot 379 Derby 1928.*
ADM395214	QQV	CA. BTU Tool Van. Converted 1957. *Formerly LMS PI RFO (semi-open) M1027M, to dia 1707 on lot 379 Derby 1928.*

DM395223	QXX	Currock C&W Depot, Carlisle, OOU. LMR RCE Track Recording Coach. Converted 1956. *Formerly LMS PI RK M30005M, to dia 1697 on lot 65 Derby 1924.*
TDM395279	QXV	(Luton Freight Sidings). Operating Department Instruction Saloon. Converted 1958 as RCE Inspection Saloon. *Formerly LMS PIII RK M30088M, to dia 1912 on lot 956 Gloucester 1936.*
TDM395280	QXW	CJ. Operating Department Instruction Saloon. Converted 1958 as RCE Inspection Coach. *Formerly LMS PIII RK M30106M, to dia 1912 on lot 1081 Derby 1938.*
ADM395316	QXV	(IL). RM & EE OHLM Pantograph Coach. Converted 1958 as high speed pantograph test coach for EML electrification scheme. *Formerly LMS PI BG M30670M, to dia 1715 on lot 344 Cammell-Laird 1928.*
LDM395328‡	QYV	(ZD for repair). Electrification Section Workshop Coach. Converted 1957 for GSU electrification scheme. *Formerly LNWR TK M3061M to dia 133 Wolverton 1907 (Lot No. B185).*
DM395366‡	QPV	LMR. RCE Staff & Dormitory Coach. Converted 1957 for Matisa Ballast Cleaner. *Formerly LNWR BT M22697M to dia 333 Wolverton 1919 (LNWR number 7707 to Lot 321).*
ADM395375	QQV	AN. BTU Tool Van. Converted 1959 under the 1956 BTU Programme. *Formerly LMS PI TO M7799M, to dia 1353 on lot 94 Derby 1924.*
ADM395376	QQV	Toton Yard, condemned awaiting disposal to Marple and Gillott, Sheffield. BTU Tool Van. *Formerly LMS PI TO M7773M, to dia 1353 on lot 1 Derby 1925.*
KDM395377	QQV	Chester S&T Sidings. S&T Tool Van. Converted 1959 under the 1956 BTU Programme. *Formerly LMS PI TO M7785M, to dia 1353 on lot 1 Derby 1924.*
DM395378	QPV	Guide Bridge Engineers' Yard. RCE Tunnel Inspection Staff Coach. Converted 1959 under the 1956 BTU Programme. *Formerly LMS PI TO M7817M, to dia 1353 on lot 94 Derby 1924.*
DM395385	QPV	ScR. RCE Staff Coach for Ballast Cleaner DR76201. Converted 1959 under the 1956 BTU Programme. *Formerly LMS PI CK M3597M, to dia 1694 on lot 157 Derby 1925.*
ADM395389	QXV	LG. RM & EE OHLM Workshop Coach. Converted 1959 for EML Electrification Scheme. *Formerly LMS PI (MR style) TK M1221M, to dia 1756 on lot 7 Derby 1924.*
LDM395390	QYV	(ZD for repair). Electrification Section Workshop Coach. Converted 1958 for EML Electrification Scheme. *Formerly LMS PI (MR style) TK M1222M, to dia 1756 on lot 7 Derby 1924.*
ADM395393	QXV	LG. RM & EE OHLM Workshop Coach. Converted 1959 for EML Electrification Scheme. *Formerly LMS PI TK M1293M, to dia 1695 on lot 71 Derby 1924.*
DM395394	QPV	Salop Sidings, Stafford. RCE Staff Coach. Converted 1959 for EML Electrification Scheme. *Formerly LMS PI (MR style) TK M1246M, to dia 1756 on lot 7 Derby 1924.*
LDM395395	QYV	(ZD for repair). Electrification Section Staff & Office Coach. Converted 1959 for EML Electrification Scheme. *Formerly LMS PI (MR style) TK M1248M, to dia 1756 on lot 8 Derby 1924.*
LDM395396	QYV	Prescott Street OHLM Depot, Wigan. Electrification Section Generator Van. Converted 1959 for EML Electrification Scheme. *Formerly LMS PI (MR style) TK M1256M, to dia 1756 on lot 8 Derby 1924.*
LDM395397	QYV	(ZD for repair). Electrification Section Workshop & Generator Van. Converted 1958 for EML Electrification Scheme. *Formerly LMS PI (MR style) TK M1247M, to dia 1756 on lot 8 Derby 1924.*
LDM395398	QYV	(ZD for repair). Electrification Section Workshop Coach. Converted 1958 for EML Electrification Scheme. *Formerly LMS PI (MR style) TK M1233M, to dia 1956 on lot 7 Derby 1924.*
DM395399	QQV	Salop Sidings, Stafford. RCE Tool Van. Converted 1958 for EML Electrification Scheme. *Formerly LMS PI (MR style) TK M1259M, to dia 1756 on lot 8 Derby 1924.*

ADM395400	QXV	Rugby OHLM Depot. RM & EE OHLM Workshop Coach. Converted 1958 for EML Electrification Scheme. *Formerly LMS PI (MR style) TK M1218M to dia 1756 on lot 7 Derby 1924.*
ADM395401	QXV	Rugby OHLM Depot. RM & EE OHLM Workshop Coach. Converted 1958 for EML Electrification Scheme. *Formerly LMS PI (MR style) TK M1260M to dia 1756 on lot 8 Derby 1924.*
LDM395404	QYV	(ZD for repair). Electrification Section Bridge Half Deck Coach. Converted 1959 for EML Electrification Scheme. *Formerly LMS PI (MR style) TK M1261M to dia 1756 on lot 8 Derby 1924.*
ADM395405	QRV	WN. RM & EEE OHLM Stores Van. Converted 1959 for EML Electrification Scheme. *Formerly LMS PI (MR style) TK M1242M to dia 1756 on lot 8 Derby 1924.*
LDM395406	QYV	(Stowmarket). Electrification Section Bridge Half Deck Coach. Converted 1959 for EML Electrification Scheme. *Formerly LMS PI (MR style) TK M1220M to dia 1756 on lot 7 Derby 1924.*
LDM395407	QYV	(ZD for repair). Electrification Section Staff Coach. Converted 1958 for EML Electrification Scheme. *Formerly LMS PI (MR style) TK M1214M to dia 1756 on lot 7 Derby 1924.*
TDM395455	QXV	Watford Junction. Operating Department Instruction Coach. Converted 1958. *Formerly LNWR BG M32745M to dia 378C Wolverton 1916. (Former World War I Ambulance Coach - originally LNWR 8898).*
DM395459	QPV	LMR. RCE Staff & Dormitory Coach for Ballast Cleaner DR76217. Converted 1958 for Matisa Ballast Cleaner. *Formerly LMS PI CK M3529M, to dia 1694 on lot 30 Wolverton 1924.*
ADM395476	QPV	AN. BTU Staff Coach. Converted 1959. *Formerly LMS PI BCK M6618M, to dia 1754 on lot 31 Wolverton 1924.*
ADM395480	QQV	BX. BTU Tool Van. Converted 1959. *Formerly LMS PI BCK M6624M, to dia 1754 on lot 31 Wolverton 1924.*
ADM395481	QQV	TI. BTU Tool Van. Converted 1959. *Formerly LMS PI BCK M6617M, to dia 1754 on lot 31 Wolverton 1924.*
ADM395483	QQV	CD. BTU Tool Van. Converted 1959. *Formerly LMS PI BCK M6614M, to dia 1754 on lot 31 Wolverton 1924.*
CDM395489	QRV	Northampton Yard. BREL Stores Van (Cells). Condemned. Converted 1958. *Formerly LMS CCT M35054M, to dia 1871 on lot 111 Wolverton 1926.*
CDM395490	QRV	Northampton Goods. BREL Stores Van (Cells). OOU. Converted 1958. *Formerly LMS CCT M35060M, to dia 1871 on lot 123 Wolverton 1926.*
CDM395491	QRV	Northampton Yard. BREL Stores Van (Cells). Condemned. Converted 1958. *Formerly LMS CCT M35127M, to dia 1871 on lot 123 Wolverton 1926.*
CDM395492	QRV	ZN. BREL Stores Van (Cells). Converted 1958. *Formerly LMS CCT M35062M, to dia 1871 on lot 123 Wolverton 1926.*
KDM395498	QPV	Marylebone, condemned awaiting disposal to Marple and Gillott, Sheffield. S&T Staff & Dormitory Coach. Converted 1959. *Formerly LMS PI TK M1295M to dia 1695 on lot 71 Derby 1924.*
ADM395526	QXV	(IL). RM & EE OHLM Generator Van. Converted 1959. *Formerly LMS PI BG M30659M to dia 1715 on lot 344 Cammell-Laird 1928.*
CDM395569	QRV	Northampton Yard. BREL Stores Van (Cells). Condemned. Converted 1960. *Formerly LMS CCT M35121M, to dia 1871 on lot 123 Wolverton 1926.*
CDM395570	QRV	Northampton Yard. BREL Stores Van (Cells). Condemned. Converted 1960. *Formerly LMS CCT M35036M, to dia 1871 on lot 111 Wolverton 1926.*
LDM395608	QYV	(KD). Electrification Section Workshop Coach. Converted 1960. *Formerly LMS PII TO M7730M to dia 1795 on lot 522 Derby 1930.*
ADM395610	QQV	Salop Sidings, Stafford. RM & EE OHLM Tool Van. Converted 1960. *Formerly LMS PI RTO M7641M, to dia 1699 on lot 156 Derby 1925.*
LDM395612	QYV	Wigan Bamfurlong Sidings. OOU. Electrification Section Stores Van. Converted 1960. *Formerly LMS PI TO M7842M, to dia 1692 on lot 154 Derby 1925.*
ADM395614	QXV	Rugby OHLM Depot. RM & EE OHLM Staff Coach. Converted 1960. *Formerly LMS PI TO M8116M, to dia 1692 on lot 302 Derby 1927.*

LDM395615 QYV (ZD for repair). Electrification Section Workshop Coach. Converted 1960.
Formerly LMS PII TO M8727M, to dia 1807 on lot 597 Wolverton 1931.

ADM395617 QXV Rugby OHLM Depot. RM & EE OHLM Workshop Coach. OOU. Converted 1960.
Formerly LMS PI TO M8161M, to dia 1692 on lot 302 Derby 1927.

ADM395618 QRV Rugby OHLM Depot. RM & EE OHLM Stores Van. Converted 1960.
Formerly LMS PII RTO M9044M, to dia 1721 on lot 519 Derby 1930.

LDM395619 QYV (ZD for repair). Electrification Section Stores Coach. Converted 1960, refurbished on lot 3823, 1971.
Formerly LMS PI FO M7447M, to dia 1742 on lot 293 Derby 1926.

ADM395620 QXV Rugby OHLM Depot. RM & EE Workshop Coach. Converted 1960.
Formerly LMS PI TO M7873M, to dia 1692 on lot 154 Derby 1925.

ADM395621 QXV Rugby OHLM Depot. RM & EE OHLM Workshop Coach. Converted 1960.
Formerly LMS PI TO M8108M, to dia 1692 on lot 302 Derby 1927.

ADM395622 QXV BY. RM & EE OHLM Workshop Coach. Converted 1960.
Formerly LMS PI TO M8097M, to dia 1692 on lot 302 Derby 1927.

LDM395623 QYV (GW). Electrification Section Workshop Coach. Converted 1960, refurbished on lot 3823, 1971.
Formerly LMS PI FO M7442M, to dia 1742 on lot 293 Derby 1926.

ADM395624 QRV Salop Sidings, Stafford. RM & EE OHLM Stores Van. Converted 1960.
Formerly LMS PI TO M8102M, to dia 1692 on lot 302 Derby 1927.

The following are RM & EE OHLM workshop coaches (QXV) and were converted in 1960/1 from LMS PI TOs to dia 1692:

No.	*Location*	*Formerly*	*Build Details*
ADM395625	Rugby OHLM Depot	M8245M	Lot 343 Derby 1928
ADM395626	BY	M8284M	Lot 355 Derby 1928
ADM395627	SI	M8437M	Lot 375 Derby 1928
ADM395628	LG	M8105M	Lot 302 Derby 1927
ADM395629	Rugby OHLM Depot	M8232M	Lot 343 Derby 1928
ADM395630	Rugby OHLM Depot	M8481M	Lot 431 Derby 1929

ADM395631 QRV SP. RM & EE OHLM Stores Van. Converted 1961.
Formerly LMS PII TO M8843M, to dia 1807 on lot 654 Derby 1932.

ADM395632 QXV SI. RM & EE OHLM Pantograph & Workshop Coach. Converted 1961.
Formerly LMS PI TO M8487M, to dia 1692 on lot 431 Derby 1929.

ADM395633 QXV Rugby OHLM Depot. RM & EE OHLM Workshop Coach. Converted 1961.
Formerly LMS PI FO M7425M, to dia 1742 on lot 155 Derby 1926.

ADM395635 QXV WN. RM & EE OHLM Workshop Coach. Converted 1961.
Formerly LMS PI TO M8409M, to dia 1692 on lot 375 Derby 1928.

ADM395636 QPV Rugby OHLM Depot. RM & EE OHLM Staff Coach. Converted 1960.
Formerly LMS PI CK M3770M, to dia 1716 on lot 450 Wolverton 1930.

ADM395637 QPV Rugby OHLM Depot. RM & EE OHLM Staff Coach. OOU. Converted 1960.
Formerly LMS PI TK M1282M, to dia 1695 on lot 71 Derby 1924.

ADM395639 QPV SI. RM & EE OHLM Staff & Office Coach. Converted 1960.
Formerly LMS PI CK M3570M, to dia 1694 on lot 120 Wolverton 1925.

The following are workshop coaches converted in 1960 from LMS PI vehicles, belonging to the RM & EE (QXV), except those with L prefixes which belong to the Electrification Section, BRB and are coded QYV:

No.	*Location*	*Formerly*	*Type*	*Dia*	*Build Details*
LDM395641	Prescot Street OHLM Depot, Wigan	M3742M	CK	1716	Lot 450 Wolverton 1930
ADM395643	Rugby OHLM Depot	M3757M	CK	1716	Lot 450 Wolverton 1930
ADM395644	(GW)	M5032M	BFK	1654	Lot 326 Derby 1927
ADM395646	CE	M3589M	CK	1694	Lot 157 Derby 1925
LDM395652	(Stowmarket)	M7637M	RTO	1699	Lot 156 Derby 1925
LDM395654	(ZD for repair)	M3740M	CK	1716	Lot 450 Wolverton 1930

LDM395657 QYV (ZD for repair). Electrification Section Pantograph Coach. Converted 1960.
Formerly LMS PI CK M3758M, to dia 1716 on lot 450 Wolverton 1930.

LDM395658 QYV (ZD for repair). Electrification Section Pantograph Coach. Converted 1960.
Formerly LMS PI CK M3749M, to dia 1716 on lot 450 Wolverton 1930.

ADM395659 QXV SP. RM & EE OHLM Pantograph Coach. Converted 1960.
Formerly LMS Pl RTO M7652M, to dia 1699 on lot 156 Derby 1925.

LDM395673 QYV (GW). Electrification Section Staff & Office Coach. Converted 1960.
Formerly LMS Pl TK M1310M, to dia 1695 on lot 95 Derby 1920.

ADM395675 QPV CE. RM & EE OHLM Staff & Office Coach. Converted 1960.
Formerly LMS Pl TK M1304M, to dia 1695 on lot 95 Derby 1920.

ADM395677 QXV Rugby OHLM Depot. RM & EE OHLM Workshop Coach. Converted 1960.
Formerly LMS Pl TO M7874M, to dia 1692 on lot 154 Derby 1925.

ADM395678 QXV SP, condemned awaiting disposal by Texas Metal Industries, Hyde. RM & EE OHLM Workshop Coach. Converted 1960.
Formerly LMS Pl TO M8438M, to dia 1692 on lot 375 Derby 1928.

The following are workshop and generator vans, converted in 1960 from LMS Pl vehicles, belonging to the RM & EE (QXV), except those with L prefixes which belong to the Electrification Section, BRB and are coded QYV:

No.	*Location*	*Formerly*	*Type*	*Dia*	*Build Details*		
ADM395679	LG	M6671M	BCK	1755	Lot 320	Wolverton	1927
ADM395680	CE	M8192M	TO	1692	Lot 343	Derby	1927
LDM395682	(ZD for repair)	M8230M	TO	1692	Lot 343	Derby	1927
LDM395683	(ZD for repair)	M8341M	TO	1692	Lot 355	Derby	1928
LDM395684	(ZD for repair)	M7663M	RTO	1699	Lot 156	Derby	1925
ADM395685	CE	M7835M	TO	1692	Lot 154	Derby	1925

LDM395688 QYV (Stowmarket). Electrification Section Workshop Coach. Converted 1961.
Formerly LMS Pl TO M8184M, to dia 1692 on lot 343 Derby 1927.

ADM395690 QXV LG. RM & EE OHLM Workshop Coach. Converted 1961.
Formerly LMS Pl FO M7407M, to dia 1742 on lot 138 Derby 1925.

LDM395691 QYV (Stowmarket). Electrification Section Pantograph Coach. Converted 1961.
Formerly LMS Pl CO M9719M, to dia 1744 on lot 93 Derby 1925.

LDM395693 QYV (ZD for repair). Electrification Section Pantograph Coach. Converted 1961.
Formerly LMS Pl CO M9711M, to dia 1744 on lot 93 Derby 1925.

ADM395694 QXV SI. RM & EE OHLM Pantograph Coach. Converted 1961.
Formerly LMS Pl TO M8255M, to dia 1692 on lot 343 Derby 1927.

KDM395698 QPV Bescot Yard. S&T Staff & Tool Coach. OOU. Converted 1961 to replace DM395205 at Saltley).
Formerly LMS Pl TO M7768M, to dia 1353 on lot 1 Derby 1924.

TDM395707 QXX EN. LMR General Managers' Saloon. Converted 1961.
Formerly LMS Pl BFK M5033M, to dia 1654 on lot 326 Derby 1927. Body Mounted onto U/F of BR Mk1 M43232, to dia 371 on lot 30093 Doncaster 1954 and fitted with B4 bogies, Wolverton 1965.

LDM395708 QYV (ZD for repair). Electrification Section Staff & Office Coach. Converted 1961.
Formerly LMS Pl CK M3548M, to dia 1694 on lot 72 Wolverton 1925.

LDM395709 QYV (ZD for repair). Electrification Section Staff & Office Coach. Converted 1961.
Formerly LMS Pl TK M1433M, to dia 1695 on lot 388 Wolverton 1928.

ADM395710 QPV LG. RM & EE OHLM Staff & Office Coach. Converted 1961.
Formerly LMS Pl TK M1487M, to dia 1695 on lot 388 Wolverton 1928.

ADM395711 QPV Rugby OHLM Depot. RM & EE OHLM Staff & Office Coach. OOU. Converted 1961.
Formerly LMS Pl TK M1290M, to dia 1695 on lot 71 Derby 1924.

ADM395713 QXV Rugby OHLM Depot. RM & EE OHLM Workshop & Generator Van. OOU. Converted 1961.
Formerly LMS Pl FO M7438M, to dia 1742 on lot 293 Derby 1926.

ADM395714 QXV Rugby OHLM Depot. RM & EE OHLM Workshop & Generator Van. Converted 1961.
Formerly LMS Pl BTK M5226M, to dia 1696 on lot 145 Derby 1926.

ADM395715 QXV SI. RM & EE OHLM Workshop & Generator Van. Converted 1961.
Formerly LMS Pl TO M7777M, to dia 1353 on lot 1 Derby 1924.

The following are workshop coaches, converted in 1961 from LMS Pl vehicles, belonging to the RM & EE (QXV), except those with L prefixes which belong to the Electrification Section, BRB and are coded QYV.

No.	Location	Formerly	Type	Dia	Build Details		
LDM395716	Prescot Street OHLM Depot, Wigan	M1018M	FK	1748	Lot 325	Wolverton	1927
ADM395717	LG	M3569M	CK	1694	Lot 120	Wolverton	1925
LDM395718	(ZD for repair)	M6683M	BCK	1755	Lot 320	Wolverton	1927
LDM395720	(KD)	M3588M	CK	1694	Lot 157	Derby	1925

The following are pantograph coaches, converted in 1961 from LMS PI vehicles belonging to the Electrification Section, BRB (QYV), except ADM395724 which belongs to RM & EE (QXV):

No.	Location	Formerly	Type	Dia	Build Details		
ADM395724	WN	M8446M	TO	1692	Lot 375	Derby	1928
LDM395725	Prescot Street OHLM Depot, Wigan	M1231M	TK	1756	Lot 7	Derby	1924
LDM395726	(ZD for repair)	M3581M	CK	1694	Lot 120	Wolverton	1925
LDM395728	(ZH for repair)	M6649M	BCK	1755	Lot 208	Wolverton	1926

ADM395753 QPV SP. BTU Staff Coach. Converted 1961 under the 1959 BTU Programme.
Formerly LMS PI BTK M5225M, to dia 1696 on lot 125 Derby 1926.

ADM395754 QPV CH. BTU Staff Coach. Converted 1961 under the 1959 BTU Programme, for WN.
Formerly LMS PI BCK M6650M, to dia 1755 on lot 208 Wolverton 1926.

ADM395757 QPV KD. BTU Staff Coach. OOU. Converted 1962 under the 1959 BTU Programme.
Formerly LMS PI BTK M5243M, to dia 1696 on lot 125 Derby 1926.

ADM395762 QQV BY. BTU Tool Van. Converted 1962 under the 1959 BTU Programme.
Formerly LMS PI CK M3595M, to dia 1694 on lot 157 Derby 1925.

KDM395767 QQV Chester S&T Sidings. S&T Tool Van. Converted 1962 under the 1959 BTU Programme.
Formerly LMS PI BTK M5291M, to dia 1696 on lot 148 Derby 1926.

DM395791 QPV Derby St. Marys. RCE Staff & Tool Coach. Condemned. Converted 1962 for Ballast Cleaner.
Formerly LMS PI TO M8301M, to dia 1692 on lot 355 Derby 1928.

DM395798 QPV (Llandeilo Jct). RCE Staff & Dormitory Coach latterly for Viaduct Inspection Unit DR82101. OOU. Converted 1962.
Formerly LMS PI TK M1428M, to dia 1695 on lot 388 Wolverton 1928.

DM395799 QPV LMR. RCE Staff & Dormitory Coach for Ballast Cleaner DR76207. Converted 1962.
Formerly LMS PI TK M1451M, to dia 1695 on lot 388 Wolverton 1928.

DM395802 QPV LMR. RCE Staff & Dormitory Coach for Ballast Cleaner DR76216. Converted 1962.
Formerly LMS PI CK M3751M, to dia 1716 on lot 450 Wolverton 1930.

DM395812 QPV LMR. RCE Staff & Dormitory Coach for Twin Jib Crane DRC78228. Converted 1962.
Formerly LMS PI TK M1307M, to dia 1695 on lot 95 Derby 1925.

DM395814 QPV LMR. RCE Staff & Dormitory Coach for Twin Jib Crane DRP78211. Converted 1962 to replace DM198649.
Formerly LMS PIII CK M3848M, to dia 1859 on lot 694 Wolverton 1933.

DM395815 QPV LMR. RCE Staff & Dormitory Coach for Twin Jib Crane DRS78204. Converted 1962 to replace DM395040.
Formerly LMS PII CK E3820M, to dia 1791 on lot 531 Wolverton 1931.

DM395816 QPV LMR. RCE Staff & Dormitory Coach for Twin Jib Crane DRC78238. Converted 1962 to replace DM395178.
Formerly LMS PI CK M3760M, to dia 1716 on lot 450 Wolverton 1930.

ADM395817 QXV (Guide Bridge). Frequency Changer Coach.
Formerly LMS PII BTK M5382M, to dia 1730 on lot 542 Metro-Cammell 1931.

DM395825 QPV (Grindleford). RCE Staff & Tool Coach. Converted 1962.
Formerly LMS PIII TK M1800M, to dia 1899 on lot 802 Wolverton 1934.

DM395832 QPV WB. RCE Staff & Tool Coach. OOU. Converted 1963.
Formerly LMS PIII TK M1535M, to dia 1860 on lot 695 Wolverton 1933.

ADM395838 QXV (Guide Bridge). Mobile Generator Van.
Formerly LMS CCT M35098M, to dia 1871 on lot 123 Wolverton 1926.

RDM395840	QXV	RTC, Derby. Laboratory 26 Rail Flaw Detection Coach, Originally Pantograph Observation Coach. *Formerly LMS PIII TO M9025M, to dia 1904 on lot 805 BRCW 1934.*
ADM395843	QPV	KD. BTU Staff Coach. Converted 1963 for Wellingborough MPD. *Formerly LMS PI BCK M6723M, to dia 1704 on lot 454 Wolverton 1929.*
KDM395844	QQV	Chester S&T Sidings. S&T Tool Van. Converted 1965 as BTU Tool Van for Wellinborough MPD. *Formerly LMS PI BTO M9844M, to dia 1693 on lot 303 Wolverton 1927.*
TDM395845	QPV	TO. RM & EE Staff Coach. Converted 1965. *Formerly LMS PI BCK M6720M, to dia 1704 on lot 454 Wolverton 1929.*
ADM395846	QQV	KD. BTU Tool Van. Converted 1965. *Formerly LMS PIII TK E1846M, to dia 1899 on lot 803 Wolverton 1934.*
ADM395848	QQV	CD. BTU Tool Van. Converted 1965 for Cockshute MPD, Stoke. *Formerly LMS PIII TK M1550M, to dia 1899 on lot 730 Derby 1933.*
DM395852	QPV	LMR. RCE Staff & Dormitory Coach for Twin Jib Crane DRB78112. Converted 1963. *Formerly LMS PIII TK M1775M, to dia 1899 on lot 801 Wolverton 1934.*
ADM395855	QPV	TO. BTU Staff Coach. Converted 1963. *Formerly LMS PIII BTK M5555M, to dia 1905 on lot 738 Derby 1934.*
DM395865	QXV	Watford Junction Engineers' Sidings. RCE Instruction Coach. OOU. Converted 1964. *Formerly LMS PIII BTK E5807M, to dia 1905 on lot 898 Derby 1936.*
DM395867	QPV	LMR. RCE Staff & Dormitory Coach for Twin Jib Crane DRC78236. Converted 1964. *Formerly LMS PIII BTK M5757M, to dia 1905 on lot 859 Wolverton 1935.*
DM395884	QPV	Basford Hall Yard, Crewe. RCE Staff & Dormitory Coach. Condemned. Converted 1964. *Formerly LMS PIII TK E1641M, to dia 1899 on lot 796 Derby 1934.*
DM395888	QPV	Basford Hall Yard, Crewe. RCE Dormitory Coach. Condemned. Converted 1964. *Formerly LMS PIII T M12030M, to dia 1906A on lot 1094 Wolverton 1938.*
KDM395892	QPV	West Ealing, condemned awaiting disposal to W. Smith, Wakefield. S&T Staff Coach. Converted 1964 as S&T Lecture Coach. *Formerly LMS PIII TO M9125M, to dia 1915 on lot 857 Wolverton 1935.*
DM395895	QPV	Watford Jct Engineers' Sidings. RCE Staff & Tool Coach. Converted 1964. *Formerly LMS PIII BTK M5727M, to dia 1905 on lot 859 Wolverton 1935.*
DM395896	QXV	Liverpool District. RCE Tunnel Inspection Coach. Converted 1964. *Formerly LMS PIII BTK M5752M, to dia 1905 on lot 859 Wolverton 1935.*
DM395898	QPV	North Wales. RCE Staff & Tool Coach. Converted 1965. *Formerly LMS PIII BTK M5734M, to dia 1905 on lot 859 Wolverton 1935.*
DM395899	QPV	Watford Junction Engineers' Sidings. RCE Staff & Tool Coach. *Formerly LMS PIII BTK M5815M, to dia 1905 on lot 898 Derby 1936.*
DM395906	QPV	North Wales. RCE Staff & Tool Coach. Converted 1965. *Formerly LMS PIII BTK SC5589M, to dia 1905 on lot 739 Wolverton 1934.*
DM395912	QPV	LMR. RCE Staff & Dormitory Coach for Twin Jib Crane DRB78121. Converted 1965. *Formerly LMS PIII T M11915M, to dia 1906A on lot 1043 Wolverton 1937.*
DM395918	QPV	Slateford Engineers' Yard. RCE Staff & Tool Coach. Converted 1965. *Formerly LMS PII T Sc11406M, to dia 1784 on lot 523 Derby 1930.*
ADM395919	QPV	BX. BTU Staff & Tool Coach. Converted 1965. *Formerly LMS PIII BTK M5822M, to dia 1905 on lot 899 Derby 1936.*
ADM395923	QQV	NH. BTU Tool Van. Converted 1965. *Formerly LMS PIII TO M9205M, to dia 1915 on lot 894 Derby 1936.*
ADM395924	QQV	BS. BTU Tool Van. Converted 1964. *Formerly LMS PIII TO M9347M, to dia 1915 on lot 954 BRCW 1936.*
ADM395926	QPV	Chester S&T Sidings. BTU Staff Coach. OOU. Converted 1965. *Formerly LMS PIII BTK M26311M, to dia 1968 on lot 1192 Wolverton 1939.*
ADM395945	QQW	TO. BTU Tool Van. *Formerly LMS PIII TO M27219M, to dia 1999 on lot 1401 Wolverton 1945.*

ADM395946 QQV CD. BTU Tool Van. Converted 1967.
Formerly LMS PIII TO M27253M, to dia 1999 on lot 1402 Wolverton 1947.

ADM395947 QSV IS. Steam Heating Boiler Van.
Formerly LMS PI TO M8043M, to dia 1745 on lot 185 Metro C&W 1926. Renumbered W44409M upon conversion 1960, renumbered 1966.

DM395951 QQV York Leeman Road Engineers' Yard. RCE Tool Van. Converted 1966 for NE Region.
Formerly LMS CCT M35527M, to dia 1929 on lot 860 Wolverton 1935.

The following vehicles are RM & EE OHLM cable drum carriers (QVV), converted in 1967 from LMS (or LMS design) PIII vehicles:

No.	*Location*	*Formerly*	*Type*	*Dia*	*Build Details*		
ADM395956	CE	M2278M	TK	2119	Lot 1407	Derby	1946
ADM395957	BY	M2160M	TK	2119	Lot 1405	Derby	1946
ADM395960	Rugby OHLM Depot	M2199M	TK	2119	Lot 1405	Derby	1946
ADM395961	SI	M2210M	TK	2119	Lot 1406	Derby	1946
ADM395965	Prescot Street OHLM Depot, Wigan	M2266M	TK	2119	Lot 1407	Derby	1946
ADM395966	CE	M16753M	C	1921A	Lot 1449	Derby	1946
ADM395967	CE	M15895M	T	2124	Lot 1578	Wolverton	1950
ADM395968	BY	W2296M	TK	2119	Lot 1407	Derby	1946
ADM395970	Salop Sidings, Stafford	M15875M	T	2124	Lot 1451	Derby	1949
ADM395972	Salop Sidings, Stafford	M27330M	TO	1999	Lot 1402	Wolverton	1947
ADM395974	SI	M27298M	TO	1999	Lot 1402	Wolverton	1947

LDM395980 QYV (ZD for repair). Electrification Section Staff & Office Coach. Converted 1968, refurbished on lot 3775 1971.
Formerly LMS PIII BTK M26379M, to dia 1968 on lot 1409 Derby 1945.

DM395982 QPV Crewe South Yard. RCE Staff & Dormitory Coach. OOU. Converted 1969.
Formerly LMS PIII TK M1711M, to dia 1899 on lot 799 Derby 1934.

KDM395992 QPV HD. S&T Staff & Tool Coach. Converted 1968.
Formerly LMS PIII BTK M26511M, to dia 1968 on lot 1410 Derby 1946.

DM395995 QPW Woking PAD. RCE Staff & Tool Coach. Converted 1969.
Formerly LMS PIII CK W4850M, to dia 2117 on lot 1440 Wolverton 1947.

KDM395997 QPV Edge Hill Sidings, condemned awaiting disposal to W. Smith, Wakefield. S&T Staff & Tool Coach. Converted 1968.
Formerly LMS PIII BTK M26322M, to dia 1968 on lot 1408 Derby 1945.

TDM395999 QRV EN. Refuse Disposal Van. Converted 1968.
Formerly LMS PMV M37754M, to dia 1870 on lot 750 Wolverton 1934.

ADM396008‡ ZSP (ZE where crane awaits conversion to diesel). Runner for Steam Crane ADRC95221.

ADM396009 QXV Brent Sidings. RM & EE Office Coach. OOU. Converted 1969.
Formerly LMS PI TO M8290M, to dia 1692 on lot 355 Derby 1928. Previously IU 023083.

Stores Unit no. 024 (ADB975250/1) is seen in Stewarts Lane depot on 7th May 1977.
[Keith Gunner

DS70120, a staff and tool coach is seen at Woking on 28th April 1981. This vehicle was converted from a Maunsell BTK.
[Keith Gunner

DS NUMBER SERIES

The current fleet of DS vehicles is split into two numbering series, those numbered between DS2 and ADS3202 and the DS70xxx series. The DS2-ADS3202 series is not in fact a list of numbers allocated in order, but a series of numbers containing many different sequences, each one current for only a few years before being abandoned in favour of another series of numbers. Some of the lower numbers have been used two or three times and those still surviving from DS2 to ADS232 were taken into departmental stock between 1953 and 1963. However the conversion of DS784 dates back to 1948. At the end of 1957 the DS70xxx series commenced and it is believed to have been chosen because the highest numbered Southern Region wagons were in the 60,000s. The highest number allocated in the DS70xxx series was DS70325 and this series of number was last used in 1971.

A marvellous variety of stock remain with Maunsell coaches well represented, while some Bulleid coaches also survive. Particularly worthy of mention is the fact that examples of the LSWR and SECR still survive. The two oldest coaches in current Southern Region departmental stock are ADS226/31, both vehicles having originally been built in July 1921 as Ironclad TK 717 and Ironclad BTK 3182 respectively. The name "Ironclad" is derived from the fact that they were steel clad, the LSWR ones being identifiable by their plate frames which with their massive construction gives the coaches a heavy look. Both coaches were withdrawn from revenue earning service in October 1957, duly entering departmental service in December 1958 and August 1959 respectively. So both have completed over 25 years of departmental service and 63 years of existence. Instead of lot numbers, the Southern used "Rolling Stock Construction Orders," normally abbreviated to RSCO.

DS2	QPW	SR. RCE Staff & Tool Van for Twin Jib Crane DRS78209. Converted 1953 for S&T. *Formerly PMV S1209S, to dia 3103 on RSCO A824 Ashford 1934.*
ADS3	QRV	Basingstoke. RM & EE Stores Van. Condemned. Converted 1953. *Formerly PMV S1187S, to dia 3103 on RSCO A824 Ashford 1936.*
ADS4	QQV	SL. BTU Tool Van. Converted 1953 for S&T. *Formerly PMV S1189S, to dia 3103 on RSCO A824 Ashford 1936.*
KDS13	QPV	(New Cross Gate C&W Shops). S&T Staff & Tool Van. Converted 1954. *Formerly PMV S1235S, to dia 3103 on RSCO A824 Ashford 1936.*
DS31	QPW	(New Cross Gate C&W Shops). RCE Staff & Tool Van. Converted 1955. *Formerly PMV S1215S, to dia 3103 on RSCO A824 Ashford 1936.*
DS36‡	QPW	(New Cross Gate C&W Shops). RCE Staff & Tool Van. Converted 1956. *Formerly PMV S2181S, to dia 3103 on RSCO A Ashford 1933.*
DS90	QPW	Hither Green PAD. RCE Staff & Tool Van. Converted 1956. *Formerly PMV S1192S, to dia 3103 on RSCO A824 Ashford 1936.*
KDS101	QPV	CJ. S&T Staff & Tool Van. Converted 1956. *Formerly PMV S2191S, to dia 3103 on RSCO A 1934.*
DS143	QQV	Woking PAD. RCE Tool Van. Converted 1954. *Formerly PMV S1233S, to dia 3103 on RSCO A824 Ashford 1936.*
ADS144	QPV	(Woking Yard). PSS Staff & Tool Van. Condemned. Converted 1954 for RCE. *Formerly PMV S1245S, to dia 3103 on RSCO A825 Ashford 1936.*
DS146	QPW	Ashford PAD. RCE Staff & Tool Van. Converted 1954. *Formerly PMV S1211S, to dia 3103 on RSCO A824 Ashford 1936.*
DS149	QPW	Eastleigh PAD. RCE Staff & Tool Van. Converted 1954. *Formerly PMV S1162S, to dia 3103 on RSCO A824 Ashford 1936.*
ADS151‡	QVV	(New Cross Gate C&W Shops). Pooley Weighing Machine Contractors' Staff & Tool Van. Converted 1956 for S&T. *Formerly PMV S2182S, to dia 3103 on RSCO A Ashford 1933.*
ADS154	QRW	New Cross Gate C&W Shops. RM & EE Stores Van. Converted 1956 for S&T. *Formerly PMV S1240S, to dia 3103 on RSCO A824 Ashford 1936.*
DS156	QPW	SR. RCE Staff & Tool Van for Twin Jib Crane DRP78222. Converted 1956 for S&T. *Formerly PMV S1156S, to dia 3103 on RSCO A824 Ashford 1936.*
DS157	QPW	SR. RCE Staff & Tool Van for Twin Jib Crane DRS78208. Converted 1957 for S&T. *Formerly PMV S1206S, to dia 3103 on RSCO A824 Ashford 1936.*

KDS160	QPV	Ashford PAD. S&T Staff & Tool Van. Converted 1957. *Formerly PMV S1249S, to dia 3103 on RSCO A824 Ashford 1936.*
KDS164	QPV	Wimbledon Engineers' Yard. S&T Staff & Tool Van. Converted 1957. *Formerly PMV S1184S, to dia 3103 on RSCO A824 Ashford 1936.*
ADS165	QPV	Horsham. PSS Staff & Tool Van. Converted 1958 for S&T. *Formerly PMV S1160S, to dia 3103 on RSCO A824 Ashford 1936.*
DS166	QPW	SR. RCE Staff & Tool Van for Twin Jib Crane DRP78216. Converted 1957. *Formerly PMV S1193S, to dia 3103 on RSCO A824 Ashford 1936.*
DS167	QPW	Woking PAD. RCE Staff & Tool Van. Converted 1957. *Formerly PMV S1216S, to dia 3103 on RSCO A824 Ashford 1936.*
DS169‡	QPW	(New Cross Gate C&W Shops). RCE Staff & Tool Van. Converted 1957. *Formerly PMV S2202S, to dia 3103 on RSCO A Ashford 1934.*
ADS225	QQV	BM. BTU Tool Van. Converted 1958. *Formerly LSWR IRONCLAD TK S724S, to dia 24 Eastleigh 1923.*
ADS226	QPV	BM. BTU Staff Coach. Converted 1958. *Formerly LSWR IRONCLAD TK S717S, to dia 24 Eastleigh 1921.*
ADS227	QQV	WD. BTU Tool Van. Converted 1958. *Formerly LSWR design IRONCLAD FK S7200S, to dia 476 Eastleigh 1924.*
ADS228	QPV	WD. BTU Staff Coach. Converted 1958. *Formerly LSWR IRONCLAD TK S730S, to dia 24 Eastleigh 1923.*
ADS229	QQV	HG. BTU Tool Van. Converted 1959. *Formerly LSWR design IRONCLAD TK S748S, to dia 24 Eastleigh 1924.*
ADS230	QPV	HG. BTU Staff Coach. Converted 1958. *Formerly LSWR design IRONCLAD TK S753S, to dia 24 Eastleigh 1924.*
ADS231	QPV	CJ. BTU Staff & Tool Coach. Condemned. Converted 1959. *Formerly LSWR IRONCLAD BTK S3182S, to dia 135 Eastleigh 1921.*
ADS232	QPV	BI. BTU Staff & Tool Coach. Converted 1959. *Formerly LSWR IRONCLAD BTK S3198S, to dia 135 Eastleigh 1923.*
ADS455	ZTV	(Tonbridge). PSS Brake Van. Converted 1957 for SR Weedkilling Train. *Formerly BRAKE VAN S55719S, built 1934.*
DS784‡	QPV	Exeter Division. RCE Staff & Dormitory Van for Crane DRP81514. Converted 1948. *Formerly SECR PMV S1998S, built 1922.*
ADS796	QXV	Basingstoke. ODM Generator Van. Condemned. Converted 1950 for RCE. *Formerly PMV S1210S, to dia 3103 on RSCO A824 Ashford 1936.*
DS798	QPW	Eastleigh PAD. RCE Staff & Tool Van. Converted 1950. *Formerly PMV S1172S, to dia 3103 on RSCO A824 Ashford 1936.*
DS800	QPW	Three Bridges PAD. RCE Staff & Tool Van for Crane DRP81517. Converted 1950. *Formerly PMV S1228S, to dia 3103 on RSCO A824 Ashford 1936.*
DS801	QPW	SR. RCE Staff & Tool Van for Twin Jib Crane DRP78223. Converted 1950. *Formerly PMV S1205S, to dia 3103 on RSCO A824 Ashford 1936.*
DS807	QPW	Three Bridges PAD. RCE Staff & Tool Van. Converted 1950. *Formerly PMV S1246S, to dia 3103 on RSCO A824 Ashford 1936.*
DS810	QPV	Taunton Engineers' Yard. RCE Staff & Tool Van. Converted 1950. *Formerly PMV S2227S, to dia 3103 on RSCO A824 Ashford 1935.*
ADS1035		Ashford Crane Shop. ODM Staff & Tool Van, coupled to Generator Van ADS1459. Converted 1948 for ODM, IoW. *Formerly SECR PMV S2012S, built 1922.*
DS1385	QPW	Woking PAD. RCE Staff & Tool Van. Converted 1949. *Formerly PMV S1350S, to dia 3103 on RSCO A824 Ashford 1939.*
ADS1459	ZXV	Ashford Crane Shop. ODM Generator Van, coupled to ADS1035. Converted 1939 for use at Herne Hill. *Formerly COVERED VAN S49445S.*
ADS3087	ZSV	SL. Match Wagon for BTU Crane ADRR95225. Built 1927.
ADS3088	ZSV	SL. Match Wagon for BTU Crane ADRR95201. Built 1927.

ADS3094	ZSV	HG. Match Wagon for BTU Crane ADRR95209. Built 1940.
ADS3095	ZSV	BI. Match Wagon for BTU Crane ADRR95210. Built 1940.
DS3141	QSV	Crofton Engineers Yard. Runner for Crane DRC80115. Converted to Stores Van 1696s further converted as Crane Runner. *Formerly SECR FK S7258S, to SR dia 486 Ashford 1904.*
ADS3202	ZXV	SE, condemned awaiting disposal on site by Allen Industries, East Finchley. Test Unit, for DEMU Stock. Constructed on U/F of LBSCR TENDER T424, built 1880.
DS70000‡	QXV	Sandown, IoW. RCE 'Britannia' Rail Loading Vehicle. Converted 1959 as compressor wagon, further converted 1981. *Formerly LSWR T S353S.*
ADS70004	QPV	(New Cross Gate C&W Shops). ODM Staff & Tool Van. Converted 1958. *Formerly PMV S1174S, to dia 3103 on RSCO A824 Ashford 1936.*
ADS70006	QPV	Horsham. PSS Staff & Tool Van. Converted 1958. *Formerly PMV S1213S, to dia 3103 on RSCO A824 Ashford 1936.*
ADS70011	QPV	BI. BTU Staff Coach. Converted 1960. *Formerly LSWR design IRONCLAD TK S728S, to dia 24 Eastleigh 1924.*
ADS70012	QPV	SL. BTU Staff Coach. Converted 1960. *Formerly LSWR design IRONCLAD TK S746S, to dia 24 Eastleigh 1924.*
ADS70014	QQV	BI. BTU Tool Van. Converted 1960. *Formerly LSWR design IRONCLAD TK S752S, to dia 24 Eastleigh 1924.*
ADS70015	QQV	SL. BTU Tool Van. Converted 1960. *Formerly LSWR design IRONCLAD TK S756S, to dia 24 Eastleigh 1925.*
ADS70020‡	QXV	Dorset Siding, Eastleigh. ODM Generator Van. Converted 1958. *Formerly PMV S2208S, to dia 3103 on RSCO 1935.*
DS70037‡	QPW	SR. RCE Staff & Tool Van for Twin Jib Crane DRS78207. Converted 1959. *Formerly PMV S2228S, to dia 3103 on RSCO 1935.*
ADS70040‡	QXV	Haywards Heath. RM & EE Office Coach. Converted 1959 as General Managers' Instruction Saloon. *Formerly Maunsell BTK S3579S, to dia 165 Eastleigh 1925.*
ADS70050	EZ5E	BI. RM & EE De-Icing Coach. Converted 1959. *Formerly 4-Sub Augmentation TS S10392S, to dia 947.*
ADS70051	EZ5E	BM. RM & EE De-Icing Coach. Converted 1959. *Formerly 4-Sub Augmentation TS S10399S, to dia 947.*
DS70055	QQW	Woking PAD. RCE Tool Van. Converted 1959. *Formerly PMV S2212S, to dia 3103 on RSCO A824 Ashford 1935.*
DS70056	QPV	WR. RCE Staff & Dormitory Van. Converted 1959 to replace DS1940. *Formerly PMV S1176S, to dia 3103 on RSCO A824 Ashford 1936.*
ADS70059	QXW	EH. BTU Tool Van. Converted 1960. *Formerly PMV S2207S, to dia 3103 on RSCO A824 Ashford 1935.*
ADS70074	QRV	Basingstoke. RM & EE Stores Van. Condemned. Converted 1960. *Formerly PMV S1177S, to dia 3103 on RSCO A824 Ashford 1936.*
ADS70078	QXV	(Woking Yard). RM & EE Office Coach. Condemned. Converted 1960 as Work Study Office. *Formerly Maunsell BTK S3569S, to dia 165 Eastleigh 1925.*
ADS70079	QXV	SE. RM & EE Office Coach. Converted 1960 as Work Study Office. *Formerly Maunsell BTK S3568S, to dia 165 Eastleigh 1925.*
ADS70087	EZ5E	AF. RM & EE De-Icing Coach. Converted 1960. *Formerly 4-Sub Augmentation TS S10400S, to dia 947.*
DS70116	QPW	Woking PAD. RCE Staff & Tool Coach. Converted 1961 for Thermit Welder Gangs. *Formerly Maunsell CK S5530S, to dia 317 Lancing 1925.*
DS70120	QPW	Woking PAD. RCE Staff & Tool Coach. Converted 1961 for Thermit Welder Gangs. *Fomerly Maunsell BTK S3557S, to dia 165 Eastleigh 1924.*
ADS70121	QPV	(Plumstead). Relief BTU Staff Coach. Converted 1963 under the 1960 BTU Programme. *Fomerly Maunsell CK S5595S, to dia 2304 1929.*

ADS70122	QPV	AF. BTU Staff Coach. Converted 1963 under the 1960 BTU Programme. *Formerly Maunsell CK S5579S, to dia 2304 1932.*
ADS70123	QPV	Horsham. PSS Staff Coach. Previously IUO83233. Converted 1963 under the 1960 BTU Programme. *Formerly LSWR design IRONCLAD TK S750S, to dia 24 Eastleigh 1924.*
ADS70124	QPV	(Perth Engineers' Yard). BTU Staff Coach. Converted 1963 under the 1960 BTU Programme. *Formerly LSWR design IRONCLAD TK S761S, to dia 24 Eastleigh 1925.*
ADS70125	QQV	(Plumstead). Relief BTU Tool Van. Converted 1962 under the 1960 BTU Programme. *Formerly Maunsell BTK S3677S, to dia 2105 Eastleigh 1929.*
ADS70126	QQV	AF. BTU Tool Van. Converted 1963 under the 1960 BTU Programme. *Formerly Maunsell BTK S3676S, to dia 2105 Eastleigh 1929.*
ADS70127	QQV	Horsham. PSS Tool Van. Previously IU083234. Converted 1963 under the 1960 BTU Programme. *Formerly LSWR IRONCLAD TK S726S, to dia 24 Eastleigh 1923.*
ADS70128	QQV	IS. BTU Tool Van. Converted 1964 under the 1960 BTU Programme. *Formerly LSWR IRONCLAD TK S747S, to dia 24 Eastleigh 1924.*
ADS70129	QPV	HG. BTU Staff & Tool Coach. Converted 1962 under the 1960 BTU Programme. *Formerly Maunsell TK S1019S, to dia 2004 Eastleigh 1934.*
ADS70130	QPV	SL. Relief BTU Staff & Tool Coach. Converted 1963 under the 1960 BTU Programme. *Formerly Maunsell TK S1023S, to dia 2004 Eastleigh 1934.*
ADS70132	QPV	Horsham. PSS Staff & Tool Coach. Converted 1960 for Lancing Works Staff Coach, as DS70061, further converted 1962 under the 1960 BTU Programme. *Formerly LSWR design IRONCLAD BTK S3208S, to dia 213 Eastleigh 1925.*
ADS70133	QPV	WD. BTU Staff & Tool Coach. Converted 1964 under the 1960 BTU Programme. *Fomrerly LSWR IRONCLAD BTK S3193S, to dia 213 Eastleigh 1923.*
ADS70154	QVW	EH. BTU Tool Van. Converted 1961 for S&T to replace DS43678. *Formerly PMV S2213S, to dia 3103 Ashford 1935.*
TDS70155	QXV	(SL). Instruction Coach. Converted 1962 as RCE Inspection Saloon to replace DS1. *Formerly Maunsell CK S5600S, to dia 2304 Eastleigh 1931.*
DS70156	QPW	SR. RCE Staff & Tool Van for Twin Jib Crane DRP78221. Converted 1962 to replace DS221. *Formerly PMV S2225S, to dia 3103 Ashford 1935.*
DS70159	QPW	SR. (SWD/CD). RCE Staff Coach for Tunnel Inspection Vehicle DM721211. Converted 1962 for Emergency Control Train Use. *Formerly Maunsell BTK S3680S, to dia 2105 Eastleigh 1929.*
ADS70161	QXV	(Brighton Top Yard). RM & EE Instruction Coach. Converted 1962 for Emergency Control Train Use. *Formerly Maunsell CK S5599S, to dia 2304 Eastleigh 1931.*
ADS70162	QXV	(New Cross Gate C&W Shops). RM & EE Office Coach. Converted 1962 for Emergency Control Train Use. *Formerly Maunsell CK S5601S, to dia 2304 Eastleigh 1931.*
ADS70163	QXV	Eastleigh Engineers' Sidings. RM & EE Office Coach. Converted 1962 for Emergency Control Train Use. *Formerly Maunsell BTK S3690S, to dia 2105 Eastleigh 1931.*
DS70164	QPW	SR (SED). RCE Tunnel Inspection Staff Coach, (with DB975663). Converted 1962 for Emergency Control Train Use. *Formerly Maunsell BTK S3691S, to dia 2105 Eastleigh 1931.*
TDS70165	QXV	Ashford Crane Shop. ODM Generator Van. Converted 1962 for Emergency Control Train Use. *Formerly SECR PMV S1996S, to dia 67/100 Ashford 1922.*

TDS70166	QXV	Ashford Crane Shop. ODM Generator Van. Converted 1962 for Emergency Control Train Use. *Formerly SECR PMV S2001S, to dia 101 Ashford 1922.*
ADS70185	ZSP	IM. Steam Heating Boiler Van. Constructed 1962 on Mineral Wagon U/F S40224S, to dia 1386 on RSCO A678 Ashford 1931.
ADS70188	ZSP	PC. Steam Heating Boiler Van. Constructed 1962 on Mineral Wagon U/F S40398S, to dia 1386 on RSCO A810 Ashford 1934.
ADS70190‡	QSV	OC. Steam Heating Boiler Van. OOU. *Formerly Prize Cattle Van S3716S*
DS70192	QSW	Woking PAD. Runner for Crane DRT81316. Converted 1964 for Crane DRT80130. *Formerly Maunsell BTK S3725S, to dia 2101 Eastleigh 1930.*
DS70193	QSW	Eastleigh PAD. Runner for Crane. Spare. Converted 1963 for Crane DRT80131. *Formerly Maunsell TO S1399S, to dia 2005 Eastleigh 1930.*
ADS70194	QSV	Horsham. Runner for Crane ADRS96102. Converted 1963 for Crane DRT80132. *Formerly Maunsell BTK S3732S, to dia 2102 Eastleigh 1930.*
DS70207	QXV	Bell Vale C&W Shops Wakefield. RCE Tunnel Inspection Van. Condemned. Converted 1963 as BTU Tool Van to replace DE176167. *Formerly CCT S2040S, to dia 3101 on RSCO A3702 Ashford 1951.*
ADS70210	ZZV	AF. Snowplough. *Formerly Schools Class Tender 723.*
ADS70211	ZZV	AF. Snowplough. *Formerly Schools Class Tender 731.*
DS70217	QPV	SL, condemned awaiting disposal to Kent & East Sussex Railway. RCE Staff & Tool Van. Converted 1966. *Formerly PMV S1145S, to dia 3103 on RSCO A855 Ashford 1937.*
DS70218	QPW	Hither Green PAD. RCE Staff & Tool Van. Converted 1964. *Formerly PMV S2206S, to dia 3103 on Ashford 1935.*
DS70220	QPW	(New Cross Gate C&W Shops). RCE Staff & Tool Van. Converted 1965 to replace DS134. *Formerly CCT S2051S, to dia 3101 on RSCO A3702 Ashford 1951.*
DS70222	QPV	(Woking Yard). RCE Staff & Tool Van. Conversion from Stores Van ADS70222 never completed. Condemned. *Formerly CCT S2035S, to dia 3103 on RSCO A2702 Ashford 1951.*

The following are snowploughs (ZZV) converted in 1965 from Schools class locomotive tenders:

No.	*Location*	*Former Tender*
ADS70224	EH	739
ADS70225	Redhill	715
ADS70226	Salisbury	701
ADS70227	Salisbury	729
ADS70228	EH	734
ADS70229	Redhill	733

DS70230	QPW	Hither Green PAD. RCE Staff & Tool Van. Converted 1965. *Formerly PMV S1142S, to dia 3103 on RSCO A855 Ashford 1937.*
DS70239	QPW	Eastleigh PAD. RCE Staff & Tool Van. Converted 1966 to replace DS1450. *Formerly CCT S2373S, to dia 3101 built Selhurst 1931.*
DS70242	QPW	Hither Green PAD. RCE Staff & Tool Van. Converted 1966. *Formerly CCT S2431S, to dia 3101 built Selhurst 1931.*
DS70243	QPW	SR. RCE Staff & Tool Van for Twin Jib Crane DRS78210. Converted 1966. *Formerly CCT S2423S, to dia 3101 built Selhurst 1931.*
DS70244	QPW	SR. RCE Staff & Dormitory Coach for Ballast Cleaner DR76213. Converted 1966. *Formerly LMS PIII BCK M6839M, to dia 1932 on lot 861 Wolverton 1935.*
DS70245	QPW	SR. RCE Staff & Dormitory Coach for Ballast Cleaner DR76214. Converted 1966. *Formerly LMS PIII BCK M6869M, to dia 2010 on lot 1098 Wolverton 1938.*

DS70247 QPW SR. RCE Staff & Dormitory Coach for Ballast Cleaner DR76211. Converted 1967.
Formerly LMS PIII BCK M6815M, to dia 1932 on lot 861 Wolverton 1935.

DS70249 QPW Woking PAD. RCE Staff & Tool Van. Converted 1966 as RM & EE Staff Van.
Formerly CCT S2411S, to dia 3101 Selhurst 1931.

ADS70251 QXV SR (SED). RM & EE Instruction Coach. Converted 1966.
Formerly Bulleid BTK (SO) S4008S, to dia 2123 Eastleigh 1950.

DS70252 QSW SR. Match Wagon for Ballast Cleaner DR76214. Converted 1967.
Formerly CCT S2374S, to dia 3101 Selhurst 1931.

DS70253 QSW SR. Match Wagon for Ballast Cleaner DR76211. Converted 1967.
Formerly CCT S2434S, to dia 3101 Selhurst 1931.

DS70254 QSW ER. Match Wagon for Ballast Cleaner DR76212. Converted 1967.
Formerly CCT S2440S, to dia 3101 Selhurst 1931.

DS70255 QSW SR. Match Wagon for Ballast Cleaner DR76213. Converted 1967.
Formerly CCT S2449S, to dia 3101 Selhurst 1931.

DS70262 QPV (Ashford PAD). RCE Tunnel Inspection Staff Coach. Converted 1967.
Formerly Bulleid RTO S1457S, to dia 2017 Eastleigh 1948.

ADS70263 QVV (Brighton Top Yard). Pooley Weighing Machine Contractors' Staff & Tool Van. Converted 1968.
Formerly CCT S2242S, to dia 3101 Selhurst 1933.

ADS70264 QVV (New Cross Gate C&W Shops). Pooley Weighing Machine Contractors' Staff & Tool Van. Converted 1968.
Formerly CCT S2497S, to dia 3101 Selhurst 1933.

ADS70268 EZ5D BM. RM & EE De-Icing Unit (930) 001. Converted 1968.
Formerly 2-Hal DMBS S10726S, to dia Eastleigh 1938.

ADS70270 EZ5D EH. RM & EE De-Icing Unit (930) 002. Converted 1968.
Formerly 4-Lav DMBS S10497S, to dia Eastleigh 1940.

ADS70272 EZ5D EH. RM & EE De-Icing Unit (930) 002. Converted 1968.
Formerly 4-Lav DMBS S10499S, to dia Eastleigh 1940.

ADS70273 EZ5D BM. EM & EE De-Icing Unit (930) 001. Converted 1968.
Formerly 4-Lav DMBS S10500S, to dia Eastleigh 1940.

The following are RCE crane runners (QSB) converted from 6-Pan EMU vehicles (70281 - 4-Res):

No.	*Crane*	*Location*	*Formerly*	*Type*	*Dia*	*Build Details*	
DS70276	DRT81338	Three Bridges PAD	S12266S	TFK	2506	RSCO Eastleigh	1935
DS70277	DRT81339	Woking PAD	S1227S	TFK	2506	RSCO Eastleigh	1935
DS70278	DRT81342	New Cross Gate PAD	S10027S	TSK	2010	RSCO Eastleigh	1935
DS70279	DRT81341	Ashford PAD	S12270S	TFK	2506	RSCO Eastleigh	1935
DS70280	DRT81340	Hither Green PAD	S11861S	TCK	2313	RSCO Eastleigh	1935
DS70281	DRT81343	Eastleigh PAD	S12235S	TFK	2506	RSCO Metro-Cammell	1937

DS70283 QPW (Folkestone East). RCE Staff & Tool Van. Converted 1969.
Formerly PMV S1359S, to dia 3101 Ashford 1939.

ADS70313 QXV BM. RM & EE Office Coach. Converted 1970. Previously IU081901.
Formerly Maunsell TO S1336S, to dia 2005 Eastleigh 1933.

AD570315 EZ5Q CJ. RM & EE Stores Unit (931) 022. OOU. Converted 1970.
Formerly 2-Hal DMBS S10731S, to dia 116 Eastleigh 1938.

ADS70316 EZ5Q FR. RM & EE Stores Unit (931) 023. OOU. Converted 1970.
Formerly 2-Hal DMBS S10742S, to dia 116 Eastleigh 1938.

ADS70317 EZ5Q FR. RM & EE Stores Unit (931) 023. OOU. Converted 1970.
Formerly 2-Hal DMBS S10760S, to dia 116 Eastleigh 1938.

ADS70318 EZ5Q CJ. RM & EE Stores Unit (931) 022. OOU. Converted 1970.
Formerly 2-Hal DMBS S10787S, to dia 116 Eastleigh 1938.

ADS70320 QXV Ashford Steelworks Sections Sidings. RM & EE Office Coach. Converted 1971.
Formerly BR Mk1 SO S3500, to dia 90 30053 Eastleigh 1953.

DS70324 QQV Wimbledon Engineers' Yard, operates on every region. Soil Mechanics' Section Tool Van. Converted 1971.
Formerly CCT S2439S, to dia 3101 on Selhurst 1931.

CDB975832, a stores van at Swindon Works, formerly Siphon G W1025W. [Keith Gunner

A former Hawksworth BG, DW150354 was used as a Cinema Coach Equipment Van. It is seen in Wolverton Works on 14th January 1973. It is now at Northampton out of use. [Keith Gunner

DW NUMBER SERIES

The current fleet of DW vehicles is split into two main groups. The first group are a mixture of survivors from various different number series and also a number of vehicles which retained their original number when taken into departmental stock. Particularly worthy of mention in this group is DW28804 which although built in 1906 still regularly moves around the Newport Division as a RCE Staff and Dormitory Van for its somewhat newer crane DRP81512 (Plasser GPC-72 5510 1979/80).

The other group is the DW150xxx series which began in 1954 and continued until ADW150432 in July 1971. However with the pending implementation of TOPS it was realised in 1972 that there were many duplicate numbers from the various earlier number series. It was decided therefore to utilise again the DW150xxx series for the required renumberings. Many of these duplicate numbers were caused by the WR practice of giving the same number to a match wagon as its parent crane. Consequently DW150433-80 were allocated to eliminate all duplicate numbers. Between 1973 and 1979 DW150481-7 were also allocated to cover either items of stock initially missed in this renumbering scheme or vehicles transferred from internal use.

Although a marvellous mixture of Churchward, Collett and Hawksworth coaches survive, of all the regional series it is the DW150xxx fleet that has been most depleted. A comprehensive history of all DW150xxx vehicles is available from our mail order department. (See section on references).

Unless stated otherwise, all DW vehicles are ex GWR or GWR design vehicles built at Swindon. Designations are as used in "Great Western Coaches 1890-1954" by Michael Harris (at present out of print).

Departmental lot numbers were issued for new or converted departmental vehicles commencing at lot 201 (formerly wagon lot 1701 of 1951) up to lot 354 of 1957 and continuing with lot 1001 of 1958 to avoid confusion with existing coaching stock lot numbers.

ADW102	ZRV	Bristol District. Sludge Tank Wagon. 3000 gall glass lined drinking water tank wagon, purchased on lot 155, 1946.
ADW104	ZRV	LA. BTU Water Tank Wagon. 3000 gall glass lined drinking water tank wagon. Purchased on lot 1555, 1946.
ADW106	ZRV	Prescott Street OHLM Depot, Wigan. RM & EE Water Tank Wagon. 3000 gall glass lined drinking water tank wagon, purchased on lot 1555, 1946.
DW139	QXX	WR. RCE Track Recording Coach. *Formerly Churchward BTK W2360, to dia D46 on lot 1174, 1911.*
DW28709	ZQV	Swindon RCE Stores Yard. Pooley Weighing Machine Contractor's Staff & Tool Van. *Formerly Mink W28709W built in 1906.*
DW28804	ZPV	Newport Division. RCE Staff and Dormitory Van for Crane DRP81512. *Formerly Mink W28804W built in 1906.*
KDW80964	ZQO	Acton Yard. S&T Tool Van. Converted on lot 1232, 1936. *Formerly MINK W26919W, to dia V12 on lot 645, 1910.*
DW80975	QXV	Bristol Barton Hill C&W Shops. RCE Bristol Division Inspection Saloon. Built to GWR dia Q13 on lot 1701, 1948.
TDW80976	QXV	Curzon Street Parcels Depot, Birmingham. Instruction Saloon. Built to GWR dia Q13 on lot 1701, 1948.
ADW123821	ZSV	IS. Steam Heating Boiler Van. Converted on lot 1069, for Plymouth Station and Millbay Docks. Constructed on U/F of MINK A W123821W, to dia V23 on lot 1125, 1933.
TDW150027	QXV	Salisbury. Exhibition Train Generator Van. Converted 1957 for Emergency Control Train Use. *Formerly SIPHON G W2790W, to dia M34 on lot 1578, 1936.*
ADW150053	QQV	LA. BTU Tool Van. Converted on lot 299, 1956 under the 1955 BTU Programme. *Formerly Churchward BTK (Multibar toplight) W3775W, to dia D56 on lot 1247, 1919.*
DW150111	QVV	White City Customs Shed, Parkeston Quay. Pooley Weighing Machine Contractor's. Staff & Tool Van. Converted on lot 323, 1956 to replace DW16912 at Truro. *Formerly BLOATER A W2115W, to dia S8 on lot 1259, 1919.*

ADW150142	ZRV	RG. Fuel Tank Wagon. Converted on lot 341, 1957 for Ranelagh Bridge Stabling Point. *Formerly Milk Tank W2501W, to dia O37, 1932.*
DW150144	QXV	Bristol Division. RCE Tunnel Inspection Staff Coach. Converted on lot 343, 1957 to replace DW258, Gloucester District. *Formerly Collett BTK (57' bow ended) W4926W, to dia D95 on lot 1375, 1927.*
DW150169	QVV	(Radyr). Pooley Weighing Machine Contractors' Staff & Tool Van. Converted on lot 351, 1957 to replace DW16906. *Formerly BLOATER W2660W, to dia S10 on lot 1356, 1925.*
DW150210	QVV	ZL. Pooley Weighing Machine Contractors Staff & Tool Van. Converted on lot 1034, 1959 to replace DW16290. *Formerly BLOATER W2240W, to dia S9 on lot 1271, 1921.*
ADW150220	QQV	RG. BTU Tool Van. Converted on lot 1044, 1959 under the 1956 BTU Programme. *Formerly Collett BTK (57' bow ended) W5125W, to dia D95 on lot 1384, 1928.*
DW150234	QPV	Northampton Yard. RCE Staff & Tool Coach. Condemned. Converted on lot 1051, 1959. *Formerly Collett BTK (57' bow ended) W5102W, to dia D95 on lot 1384, 1928.*
DW150236	QVV	Bristol Kingsland Road. Pooley Weighing Machine Contractor's Staff & Tool Van. Converted on lot 1056, 1959 to replace DW16972. *Formerly BLOATER W2625W, to dia S9 on lot 1307, 1922.*
DW150246	QPV	ZL. Staff Coach. Converted on lot 1068, 1960. *Formerly Collett BTK (57' bow ended) W5131W, to dia D95 on lot 1384, 1928.*
KDW150266	QXV	Reading. S&T Manager's Saloon. Converted on lot 1073, 1960 to replace DW45011M. *Formerly Collett RCO (57' bow ended) W9580W, to dia H33 on lot 1349, 1925. Third class saloon converted to counter buffet in 1953.*
KDW150272	QPV	Old Oak Common Siding, adjacent to signal box. S&T Staff & Tool Coach. Converted on lot 1078, 1961. *Formerly Collett BTK (57' bow ended) W5240W, to dia D104 on lot 1412, 1929.*
KDW150275	QPV	Coleham Engineers' Yard, Shrewsbury. Converted on lot 1078, 1961. *Formerly Collett TK (57' bow ended) W4887W, to dia C54 on lot 1374, 1927.*
DW150289	QPV	Taunton Engineers' Yard. RCE Bridge Department Staff & Tool Van. Converted on lot 1084, 1961 to replace DW80996 at Plymouth. *Formerly BLOATER W2661W, to dia S10 on lot 1356, 1925.*
DW150312	QQV	Bristol Marsh Jct. RCE Tool Van latterly for Ballast Cleaner DR76313. OOU. Converted on lot 1107, 1961 for Single Line Gantry Set. *Formerly FRUIT C W2826W, to dia Y9 on lot 1606, 1937.*
ADW150319	QPV	Plymouth Station. RM & EE Crane Inspectors' Staff & Dormitory Van. Converted on lot 1111, 1961 for ZL. *Formerly FRUIT D W2910W, to dia Y11 on lot 1649, 1939.*
TDW150323	QXV	Salisbury. Exhibition Train Generator Van. Converted for Emergency Control Train use. *Formerly SIPHON G W2798W, to dia M34 on lot 1578, 1936.*
DW150338	QPV	LMR. RCE Staff & Dormitory Coach for Ballast Cleaner DR76219. Converted on lot 1125, 1962. *Formerly Collett BTK (57') W5786W, to dia D116 on lot 1490, 1933.*
DW150344	QQV	Three Bridges PAD. RCE Tool Van. Converted on lot 1132, 1962. *Formerly FRUIT C W2856W, to dia Y9 on lot 1634, 1938.*
DW150349	QQV	Coleham Engineers' Yard, Shrewsbury. RCE Tool Van. Converted on lot 1134, 1962. *Formerly FRUIT C W2806W, to dia Y9 on lot 1606, 1937.*
DW150351	QVV	Bristol Kingsland Road. Pooley Weighing Machine Contractor's Staff & Tool Van. *Formerly FRUIT D W2887W, to dia Y11 on lot 1649, 1939.*
DW150352	QPV	Bristol Division. RCE Staff & Tool Van for Crane DRP81520. Converted on lot 1137, 1962 to replace Pooley Van DW82924. *Formerly BLOATER W2740W, to dia S11 on lot 1381 Contractor 1926.*

ZDW150353 QXV ZN, operates on every region. Cinema Coach. Converted 1963.
Formerly BR Mk1 RSO W1012, to dia 56 on lot 30014 York 1951.

ZDW150354 QXV Northampton Yard. Generator Van. OOU. Converted 1963.
Formerly Hawksworth BG W297W, to dia K45 on lot 1722, 1949.

DW150359 QPV WR. RCE Staff & Dormitory Coach for Ballast Cleaner DR76218. Converted 1965.
Formerly Collett BTK (61' "Sunshine") W1595W, to dia D124 on lot 1574, 1935.

DW150360 QPV WR. RCE Staff & Dormitory Coach for Trenching Unit DR85001. Converted 1965.
Formerly Collett BTK (61' "Sunshine") W1610W, to dia D124 on lot 1574, 1937.

DW150362 ZQV WR. RCE Tool Van for Single Line Gantries 78420/1. Converted 1964 for Thermit Welder Gangs.
Formerly FRUIT D W2907W, to dia Y11 on lot 1649, 1939.

DW150363 QRV Bristol East Engineers' Yard. RCE Stores Van. Converted 1964 for Thermit Welder Gangs.
Formerly Fruit D W2913W, to dia Y11 on lot 1649, 1939.

KDW150372 QPV Gloucester New Yard, condemned awaiting disposal to Cashmore, Great Bridge. S&T Staff & Tool Coach. Converted 1966.
Formerly Collett BG W670W, to dia D127 on lot 1642, 1940.

ADW150375 QXX RTC, Derby. M & EE Test Car 1. Converted 1966.
Formerly Hawksworth Auto Trailer W233W, to dia A38 on lot 1736, 1951.

The following vehicles are RCE staff & dormitory coaches (QPV) converted Wolverton 1967 (150402-7 1968) from Hawksworth BTKS built to dia D133 on lot 1732, 1950 (150407 - lot 1744, 1950). The accompanying RCE equipment is listed below (refer to 'Track Machines' for further details):

No.	*RCE Equipment*	*Location*	*Formerly*
DW150392	DR76308	WR	W2225W
DW150393	DR76209	WR	W2214W
DW150395	DR76307	WR	W2196W
DW150397	—	Reading C&W Yard. OOU.	W2232W
DW150400	78418/19	WR	W2218W
DW150401	DRP78219	WR	W2233W
DW150402	DRP78212	WR	W2216W
DW150403	78420/1	WR	W2148W
DW150404	DX50011	WR	W2220W
DW150407	—	Bristol Marsh Jct, condemned awaiting disposal to Dean Forest Railway Society, Lydney.	W2249W

DW150421 ZRV LMR. RCE Water Tank Wagon, for Drain Cleaning Train.
Formerly Shell-Mex Tank Wagon A7327, GWR registration 317 built 1940.

ADW150425 QRV ZN. RM & EE Stores Van. Converted 1969.
Formerly Horse box W2508E, on lot 1754, 1955.

ADW150444 ZSP LA. Match Wagon for BTU Crane ADRR95213.
Formerly DW19, built 1940 Ransomes & Rapier Ltd, Ipswich.

ADW150445 ZSP ZL. Match Wagon for BTU Crane, spare.
Formerly DW19A, built 1940 Ransomes & Rapier Ltd, Ipswich.

INTERNAL USERS

The very name of this category indicates quite clearly that it refers to vehicles which are not supposed to travel on running lines, but are confined to yards to depots. Within this category are many wagons, but also to be found are coaches and vans appropriated from either capital or departmental coaching stock. The lists detailed below are of all the coaches and vans to be found in the internal user fleet. Although the allocated location is normally static it is by no means unknown for internal users to be transferred from one location to another, special permission normally having to be obtained before movement can be made.

The numbering of internal user vehicles is a regional responsibility and has been so since first initiated in 1950. As will be seen from the notes below, the regions vary considerably in the effectiveness of their internal user schemes. Once the life of an internal user is over it is normally scrapped on site, although some are sent to scrapyards. Sometimes there is life after internal use the wheels and frame being scrapped but the body being grounded and used as a store. It should be noted that any internal users that so survive are not included in the lists below, but it is anticipated that the next edition of this book will include a special section on grounded coaching stock bodies formerly in capital, departmental or internal user stock.

News on additions and disposals of the internal user fleet (includng wagons) will be regularly found in the special monthly feature on departmentals in Rail Enthusiast.

The format for this section is the same as that presented in the previous sections except that the dates quoted relate to when the vehicle was transferred to the internal user fleet, whilst Carkind (TOPS) codes are not applicable.

LMR — 02xxxx

Allocated numbers have reached 024622 and vehicles have their number engraved on a plate attached to the frame, whilst the previous identity is usually obliterated.

024239 Oxley CS. Stores Van. Transferred 2/74.
Formerly BR (GWR design) Fruit D W2336W to dia Y11 on lot 1765 Swindon 1952.

024312 ZN. Stores Van. Transferred 4/77.
Formerly LMS PIII BG M31051M, to dia 2007 on lot 1260 Derby 1940.

024320 ZC. Stores Van. Transferred 5/78.
Formerly LMS design CCT W37232, to dia 2026 on lot 1770 Swindon 1957.

024379 Crewe Gresty Road Engineers' Yard. Stores Van. Transferred 11/79.
Formerly LMS CCT M35289M to dia 1872 on lot 594 Wolverton 1931.

024408 ZD. Stores Van. Transferred 4/80.
Formerly LMS PIII BG M31185M, to dia 2007 on lot 1305 Wolverton 1941.

024409 ZD. Stores Van. Transferred 4/80.
Formerly LMS PIII BG M31344M, to dia 2007 on lot 1444 Wolverton 1947.

024417 ZN. Stores Van. Transferred 12/80.
Formerly LMS PIII BG M31153M, to dia 2007 on lot 1304 Derby 1942.

024429 DY. Stores Van. Transferred 4/81.
Formerly LMS PIII BG M31338M, to dia 2007 on lot 1444 Wolverton 1947.

024430 KD. Stores Van. Transferred 3/81.
Formerly LMS PIII BG M31340M, to dia 2007 on lot 1444 Wolverton 1947.

024432 Carlisle Currock C&W Shops. Stores Van. Transferred 5/81.
Formerly LMS PIII BG M31180M, to dia 2007 on lot 1305 Wolverton 1941.

024437 Carnforth Plant Maintenance Depot. Stores Van. Transferred 5/83.
Formerly LMS design PIII BG M31421M, to dia 2171 on lot 1588 Wolverton 1950.

024445 ZD. Stores Van. Transferred 11/81.
Formerly LMS PIII BG M31231M, to dia 2007 on lot 1357 Wolverton 1944.

024450 TS. Stores Van. Transferred 8/82.
Formerly SR B S220S, to dia 3093 on RSCO L1029 Lancing/Eastleigh 1939.

024458 Crewe Gresty Road Engineers' Yard. Stores Van. Transferred 10/82.
Formerly BR Mk1 CCT M94127, to dia 816 on lot 30549 Earlestown 1959.

024460	Heysham Harbour. Staff Coach. Transferred 11/82. *Formerly BR Mk1 RB(K) M1780, to dia 46. Originally RF M323 on lot 30633 Ashford/Swindon 1961.*
024462	Heysham Harbour. Staff Coach. Transferred 11/82. *Formerly BR Mk1 TTO M3954, to dia 93 on lot 30086 Eastleigh 1954.*
024463	Nottingham London Road. Stores Van. Transferred 10/82. *Formerly BR Mk1 CCT E94474, to dia 816 on lot 30563 Earlestown 1960.*
024464	ZN. Stores Coach. Transferred 11/82. *Formerly BR Mk1 TO W3732, to dia 93 on lot 30031 Derby 1954.*
024465	RTC, Derby. Stores Van. Transferred 9/82. *Formerly SR design PMV S1478S, to dia 3103 built Wolverton 1951.*
024476	EN. Stores Coach. Transferred 8/83. *Formerly BR Mk1 RB(K) M1639 to dia 46. Converted 1970 from RF M338.*
024480	ZD. Equipment Carrier. Transferred 1/83. Previously ADM395969. *Formerly LMS PIII C M16751M, to dia 1921A on lot 1449 Derby 1949.*
024485	ZD. Equipment Carrier. Transferred 1/83. Previously ADM395971. *Formerly LMS PIII TK M2351M, to dia 2119 on lot 1406 Derby 1946.*
024486	ZD. Equipment Carrier. Transferred 1/83. Previously ADM395973. *Formerly LMS PIII TK M2245M, to dia 2119 on lot 1406 Derby 1946.*
024497	RTC, Derby. Stores and Workshop Van. Transferred 4/83. *Formerly BR Mk1 CCT W94507, to dia 816 on lot 30563 Earlestown 1960.*
024498	Aberystwyth. Staff Coach. Transferred 7/84. *Formerly BR Mk1 RBR M1749, to dia 24 on lot 30527 BRCW 1961.*
024510	CW. Stores Van. Transferred 12/83. Previously ADM40212. *Formerly LMS Fish Van M40212, to dia 2115 on lot 1428 Wolverton 1946.*
024511	CW. Stores Van. Transferred 12/83. Previously ADM40263. *Formerly LMS design Fish Van M40263, to dia 2115 on lot 1449 Wolverton 1949.*
024512	CW. Stores Van. Transferred 12/83. Previously ADM40326. *Formerly LMS design Fish Van M40326, to dia 2115 on lot 1509 Wolverton 1949.*
024515	TS. Stores Van. Transferred 5/84. *Formerly SR PMV S1897S, to dia 3103 on RSCO L1092 Lancing/Eastleigh 1940.*
024529	CW. Stores Van. Transferred 4/84. Previously ADB975795. *Formerly GWR (Hawksworth) design BG W329W, to dia K[illegible]46 on lot 1752 Swindon 1951.*
024534	Wolverhampton HL. Stores Van. To be transferred. *Formerly SR PMV S1770S, to dia 3103 on RSCO A972 Ashford/Eastleigh 1938.*
024535	Wolverhampton LL. Stores Van. Transferred 5/84. Previously TDB975996. *Formerly LMS PIII BG M31258M, to dia 2007 on lot 1357 Wolverton 1941.*
024536	TS. Stores Van. To be transferred. *Formerly SR PMV S1834S, to dia 3103 on RSCO L1092 Lancing/Eastleigh 1940.*
024604	CD. Stores Van. Transferred 6/84. Previously ADM40292. *Formerly LMS design Fish Van M40292, to dia 2115 on lot 1449 Wolverton 1949.*
024605	CD. Stores Van. Transferred 6/84. Previously ADM40300. *Formerly LMS design Fish Van M40300, to dia 2115 on lot 1509 Wolverton 1949.*
024606	Crewe Gresty Road Engineers' Yard. Stores Van. Transferred 12/84. *Formerly LMS design PIII BG M31394M, to dia 2171 on lot 1563 Derby 1949.*
024607	Preston Dock Street. Staff Coach. Transferred 8/84. *Formerly BR Mk1 RBR M1741, to dia 24 on lot 30527 BRCW 1961.*
024608	Preston Dock Street. Stores Van. Transferred 8/84. *Formerly BR Mk1 CCT M94395 to dia 816 on lot 30562 Earlestown 1960.*
024609	DY. Stores Van. To be transferred. *Formerly BR Mk1 CCT M94149 to dia 816 on lot 30549 Earlestown 1959.*
024610	DY. Stores Van. To be transferred. *Formerly BR Mk1 CCT E94605 to dia 816 on lot 30564 Earlestown 1961.*

024611	LG. Stores Van. To be transferred. *Formerly BR Mk1 CCT M94237 to dia 816 on lot 30549 Earlestown 1959.*

ER — 04xxxx

Allocated numbers have reached 041825 and although most vehicles have their old numbers painted out and the new internal user number painted on, there is an every increasing list of examples where the allocated internal user is not being applied. A number of internal users were numbered separately in the range 042xxx upwards, two of which still survive.

040877	BN. De-Greasing Coach. Transferred in 1960s. *Formerly NER FO. Precise identity unknown.*
041305	IL. Stores Coach. Transferred 7/76. Previously ADE320837. *Formerly LNER TO E12134E, to dia 27 Dukinfield 1925.*
041306	IL. Equipment Carrier. Transferred 7/76. Previously ADE320838. *Formerly LNER BTK E11045E, to dia 136 York 1928.*
041317	Norwich Thorpe Yard. Refuse Disposal Van. Transferred 5/76. Previously TDB975355. *Formerly BR Fish Van E87616, to dia 800 on lot 30344 Faverdale 1960.*
041321	Norwich Thorpe Yard. Refuse Disposal Van. Transferred 5/76. Previously TDB975359. *Formerly BR Fish Van E87602, to dia 800 on lot 30344 Faverdale 1960.*
041327	Tyneside Central Freight Depot. Cartic Ramp. Transferred 11/76. Previously TDB975092. *Formerly BR Mk1 CK SC15147, to dia 126 on lot 30005 Metro-Cammell 1952.*
041342	ZF. Stores Van. Transferred 9/77. *Formerly LNER CCT E1293E, to dia 6 York 1939.*
041343	ZF. Stores Van. Transferred 9/77. *Formerly LNER CCT E1243E, to dia 6 York 1939.*
041344	ZF. Stores Van. Transferred 9/77. *Formerly LNER CCT E1308E, to dia 6 on lot 1223 York 1950.*
041345	ZF. Stores Van. Transferred 9/77. *Formerly LMS CCT E37133E, to dia 2026 on lot 1154 Metro-Cammell 1938.*
041366	HT. Stores Van. Transferred 11/77. *Formerly LNER BGP E70754E, to dia 245 on lot 1073 York 1943.*
041369	IL. Worksop Coach. Transferred 10/77. *Formerly Class 306 DTSO E65604, to dia 363 Metro-Cammell 1949.*
041372	ZF. Stores Van. Transferred 12/77. *Formerly LNER design CCT E1340E, to dia 6 on lot 1223 York 1950.*
041405	Tyneside Central Freight Depot. Stores Van. Transferred 6/78. *Formerly GWR (Hawksworth) design BG W291W, to dia K45 on lot 1722 Swindon 1949.*
041418	Boston. RCE Staff Coach. Transferred 12/78. Previously DE320731. *Formerly (GER?) TK E61533E, to dia 419.*
041420	Norwich Thorpe yard. Stores Van. Transferred 3/78. Previously ADE87318. *Formerly BR Fish Van E87318, to dia 800 on lot 30125 Faverdale 1954.*
041426	Tyneside Central Freight Depot. Stores Van. Transferred 7/78. *Formerly GWR (Hawksworth) design BG W315W, to dia K45 on lot 1740 Swindon 1950.*
041475	SB. Tool Van. Transferred 9/79. Previously ADW87706. *Formerly BR Fish Van W87706 to dia 800, on lot 30384 Faverdale 1960.*
041486	BN. Furniture Store. Transferred 2/80. Previously ADB975556. *Formerly GWR design Fruit D W3448W, to dia Y11 on lot 1780 Swindon 1955.*
041502	ZY. Stores Van. Transferred 6/80. *Formerly LNER CCT E1371E, to dia 6 on lot 1224 York 1950.*
041503	ZF. Stores Van. Transferred 7/80. *Formerly SR PMV S1370S, to dia 3103 on RSCO A1031 Ashford 1939.*

041504	YC. Stores Van. Transferred 8/80. Previously ADE87358. *Formerly BR Fish Van E87358, to dia 800 on lot 30344 Faverdale 1960.*
041508	ZF. Stores Van. Transferred 8/80. *Formerly SR B S203S, to dia 3093 on RSCO L1029 Lancing/Eastleigh 1939.*
041526	HT. Staff Coach. Transferred 4/81. *Formerly BR Mk1 BCK E21095, to dia 171 on lot 30185 Metro-Cammell 1956.*
041541	Wakefield Kirkgate Engineers' Yard. Stores Van. Transferred 1/81. *Formerly LMS PIII BG M31100M, to dia 2007 on lot 1261 Wolverton 1940.*
041542	Wakefield Kirkgate Engineers' Yard. Stores Van. Transferred 1/81. *Formerly LMS PIII BG M31054M, to dia 2007 on lot 1260 Derby 1940.*
041543	Norwich. Stores Van. Transferred 3/81. *Formerly LMS design PIII BG M31376M, to dia 2171 on lot 1508 Wolverton 1950.*
041544	Norwich. Stores Van. Transferred 3/81. *Formerly LMS PIII BG M31047M, to dia 2007 on lot 1261 Wolverton 1940.*
041545	Huddersfield. Stores Van. Transferred 3/81. *Formerly LMS PIII BG M31227M, to dia 2007 on lot 1357 Wolverton 1944.*
041546	Wakefield Kirkgate Engineers' Yard. Stores Van. Transferred 3/81. *Formerly LMS PIII BG M31216M, to dia 2007 on lot 1357 Wolverton 1944.*
041551	ZF. Stores Van. Transferred 4/81. *Formerly SR PMV S2125S, to dia 3103 on RSCO L1191 Lancing 1942.*
041552	ZF. Stores Van. Transferred 4/81. Previously ADB975656. *Formerly GWR Siphon G W2793W, to dia M34 on lot 1578 Swindon 1937.*
041554	ZF. Boiler Van. Transferred 4/81. Previously TDE321100. *Formerly BR Mk1 Horse Box E96327 to dia 751 on lot 30146 Earlestown 1957.*
041568	Immingham Yard. Staff Coach. Transferred 7/81. Previously ADE320889. *Formerly LNER F E81052E, to dia 48 York 1927.*
041570	ZF. Stores Van. Transferred 8/81. *Formerly BR Mk1 BG M80963, to dia 711 on lot 30162 Pressed Steel 1957.*
041580	Scarborough. Stores Van. Transferred 11/81. *Formerly BR Mk1 CCT S94550, to dia 816 on lot 30563 Earlestown 1960.*
041583	Huddersfield. Stores Van. To be transferred. *Formerly LMS PIII BG M31112M, to dia 2007 on lot 1304 Derby 1941.*
041584	Wakefield Kirkgate Engineers' Yard. Stores Van. To be transferred. *Formerly LMS PIII BG M31225M, to dia 2007 on lot 1357 Wolverton 1944.*
041585	Wakefield Kirkgate Engineers' Yard. Stores Van. To be transferred. *Formerly LMS PIII BG M31333M, to dia 2007 on lot 1444 Wolverton 1947.*
041586	Wakefield Kirkgate Engineers' Yard. Stores Van. To be transferred. *Formerly LMS PIII BG M31932M, to dia 2100 on lot 1359 Wolverton 1944.*
041593	Boston. RCE Staff and Workshop Coach. To be transferred. Previously DE321089. *Formerly Camping Coach 'No. 155'. Precise identity unkown.*
041597	LN. Stores Van. Transferred 2/82. *Formerly BR Mk1 BG E80990, to dia 711 on lot 30173 York 1956.*
041605	Ferme Park Carriage Sidings, Hornsey. Staff Coach. Transferred 10/82. *Formerly BR Mk1 BCK E21219, to dia 172 on lot 30425 Metro-Cammell 1958.*
041606	Ferme Park Carriage Sidings, Hornsey. Staff Coach. Transferred 10/82. *Formerly BR Mk1 TSO E4688, to dia 93 on lot 30375 York 1957.*
041612	Zf. Stores Van. Transferred 12/82. *Formerly BR Mk1 BG M80557, to dia 711 on lot 30039 Wolverton 1954.*
041613	HM. Stores Van. Transferred 8/82. *Formerly BR Mk1 BG M81446, to dia 711 on lot 30400 Pressed Steel 1958.*
041614	Temple Mills. Stores Van. Transferred 9/82. Previously CSD70025. *Formerly SR PMV S2223S, to dia 3103 on RSCO A824 Ashford 1935.*
041618	ZF. Stores Van. Transferred 6/82. *Formerly LMS PIII BG M31220M, to dia 2007 on lot 1357 Wolverton 1944.*

041623 ZY. Stores Van. Transferred 10/82.
Formerly BR Mk1 BG E80641, to dia 711 on lot 30046 York 1954.

041624 ZY.. Stores Van. Transferred 10/82.
Formerly BR Mk1 BG M80568, to dia 711 on lot 30040 Wolveron 1954.

041625 ZY. Stores Van. Transferred 10/82.
Formerly BR Mk1 BG M80770, to dia 711 on lot 30140 BRCW 1955.

041636 ZY. Stores Van. Transferred 10/82.
Formerly BR Mk1 BG E80846, to dia 711 on lot 30144 Cravens 1955.

041637 ZY. Stores Van. Transferred 10/82.
Formerly BR Mk1 BG M81058, to dia 711 on lot 30228 Metro-Cammell 1957.

041638 Wakefield Kirkgate Engineers' Yard. Stores Van. Transferred 12/83.
Formerly BR Mk1 CCT W94522, to dia 816 on lot 30563 Earlestown 1960.

041639 Wakefield Kirkgate Engineers' Yard. Stores Van. Transferred 12/83.
Formerly BR Mk1 CCT E94496, to dia 816 on lot 30563 Earlestown 1960.

041640 Wakefield Kirkgate Engineers' Yard. Stores Van. Transferred 12/83.
Formerly BR Mk1 CCT E94630, to dia 816 on lot 30564 Earlestown 1961.

041641 Wakefield Kirkgate Engineers' Yard. Stores Van. Transferred 12/83.
Formerly BR Mk1 CCT W94589, to dia 816 on lot 30563 Earlestown 1960.

041642 Shildon. Staff Coach. Transferred 12/82.
Formerly BR Mk1 TSO E4576, to dia 93 on lot 30243 York 1956.

041643 Shildon. Staff Coach. Transferred 12/82.
Formerly BR Mk1 TSO E4490, to dia 93 on lot 30243 York 1956.

041644 MR. Stores Van. Transferred 12/82.
Formerly BR Mk1 CCT M94388, to dia 816 on lot 30562 Earlestown 1960.

041665 Shildon. Stores Van. Transferred 3/83.
Formerly BR Mk1 BG M80558, to dia 711 on lot 30039 Wolverton 1954.

041666 Shildon. Staff Coach. Transferred 3/83.
Formerly BR Mk1 TSO E4865, to dia 89 on lot 30525 Wolverton 1959.

041674 SF. Staff Coach. Transferred 8/83.
Formerly BR Mk1 TSO E4296, to dia 93 on lot 30207 BRCW 1956.

041675 SF. Staff Coach. Transferred 8/83.
Formerly BR Mk1 TSO E4408, to dia 93 on lot 30219 Ashford/Swindon 1957.

041676 Parkeston. Stores Van. Transferred 12/83.
Formerly BR Mk1 CCT S94887, to dia 816 on lot 30614 Earlestown 1961.

041678 ZF. Stores Van. Transferred 11/83.
Formerly SR design PMV S1488S, to dia 3103 built Wolverton 1951.

041682 Leyton Engineers' Yard. Stores Van. Transferred 3/84.
Formerly SR PMV S1313S, to dia 3103 on RSCO A1031 Ashford 1939.

041683 Leyton Engineers' Yard. Stores Van. Transferred 3/84.
Formerly SR design PMV S1414S, to dia 3103 on RSCO A3702 Ashford 1951.

041692 BN. Stores Van. To be transferred.
Formerly BR Mk1 CCT M94753, to dia 816 on lot 30614 Earlestown 1961.

041693 Finsbury Park. S&T Stores Van. Transferred 12/84.
Formerly BR Mk1 CCT M94102, to dia 816 on lot 30549 Earlestown 1959.

041694 Finsbury Park. S&T Stores Van. Transferred 12/84.
Formerly BR Mk1 CCT E94642, to dia 816 on lot 30564 Earlestown 1961.

041695 Darlington. RCE Stores Van. Transferred 3/84.
Formerly BR Mk1 CCT M94122, to dia 816 on lot 30549 Earlestown 1959.

041696 Darlington. RCE Stores Van. Transferred 3/84.
Formerly BR Mk1 CCT M94281, to dia 816 on lot 30549 Earlestown 1959.

041697 ZF. Stores Van. Transferred 3/84.
Formerly BR Mk1 CCT E94486, to dia 816 on lot 30563 Earlestown 1960.

041698 ZY. Stores Van. To be transferred.
Formerly BR Mk1 CCT E94456, to dia 816 on lot 30563 Earlestown 1960.

041699 ZY. Stores Van. To be transferred.
Formerly BR Mk1 CCT E94620, to dia 816 on lot 30564 Earlestown 1961.

041700	ZY. Stores Van. To be transferred. *Formerly BR Mk1 CCT W94539, to dia 816 on lot 30563 Earlestown 1960.*
041702	ZY. Stores Van. To be transferred. *Formerly BR Mk1 CCT W94592, to dia 816 on lot 30563 Earlestown 1960.*
041703	ZY. Stores Van. To be transferred. *Formerly BR Mk1 CCT E94646, to dia 816 on lot 30564 Earlestown 1961.*
041714	TE. Stores Van. To be transferred. *Formerly BR Mk1 CCT W94525, to dia 816 on lot 30563 Earlestown 1960.*
041721	DR. Stores Van. Transferred 4/84. Previously ADB975939. *Formerly LMS design PIII BG M31416M, to dia 2171 on lot 1508 Wolverton 1950.*
041722	DR. Stores Van. Transferred 4/84. Previously ADB975942. *Formerly LMS design PIII BG M31369M, to dia 2171 on lot 1508 Wolverton 1950.*
041723	Leyton Engineers' Yard. Staff Coach. To be transferred. Previously DB975800. *Formerly BR Mk1 SK E25507, to dia 146 on lot 30374 York 1958.*
041732	Wakefield C&W Shops. Office Coach. Transferred 7/84. Previously ADE320919. *Formerly LNER TO E12201E, to dia 27B York 1930 (originally 697).*
042167	Tweedmouth. Stores Van. Transferred in 1960's. *Formerly GER PMV E6037E.*
042468	TE. Staff Coach. Transferred 12/74. *Formerly BR Mk1 BSO E9291, to dia 183 on lot 30244 Doncaster 1956.*

WR — 06xxxx

Allocated numbers have reached 061051 and almost all vehicles have their number engraved on a plate attached to the frame. However, increasingly the former identity is not being obliterated which of course inevitably causes confusion, as to the casual observer it is not always apparent that the vehicle is an internal user vehicle. Various numbering blocks have been issued including 064xxx, 068xxx and 70xxx, some numbers being used more than once. Since the end of 1979 a consecutive block of numbers has been used commencing with 060900.

060904	Exeter Red Cow Crossing. S&T Contractor's Staff and Dormitory Coach. Transferred 12/79. Previously KDW9875. *Formerly Churchward TK. (Multibar toplight) W3951W to dia C35 on lot 1256, 1919.*
060905	Exeter Red Cow Crossing. S&T Contractor's Staff and Dormitory Coach. Transferred 12/79. Previously KDW9876. *Formerly Churchward TK. (Multibar toplight) W3950W to dia C35 on lot 1256, 1919.*
060907	Exeter Red Cow Crossing. S&T Contractor's Staff and Dormitory Coach. Transferrd 12/79. Previously KDW150206. *Formerly Collett TK (57' bow ended) W4777W to dia C54 on lot 1369, 1926.*
060956	MG. Fuel Tank Wagon. Transferred 1/81. Previously ADW150143. *Formerly Milk Tank W2538W, to dia O37, 1932.*
060957	Llanelli Troste Works. Stores Van. Transferred 2/81. *Formerly SR design GUV S4606S, to dia 3182 on lot RSCO L3228 Lancing 1949.*
061003	CF. First Aid Training Van. Transferred 4/82. *Formerly BR Mk1 BG M81163, to dia 711 on lot 30228 Metro-Cammell 1958.*
061022	Gloucester. RCE Stores Van. Transferred 3/84. *Formerly BR Mk1 CCT M94710, to dia 816 on lot 30614 Earlestown 1961.*
061025	Sudbrook. First Aid Training Coach. Transferred 3/84. *Formerly BR Mk1 SK W26109, to dia 146 on lot 30720 Derby 1963.*
061026	Danygraig. Stores Van. Transferred 3/84. *Formerly BR Mk1 BG E81307, to dia 711 on lot 30323 Pressed Steel 1957.*
061027	BJ. Workshop Van. Transferred 1/84. *Formerly BR Mk1 CCT M94433, to dia 816 on lot 30562 Earlestown 1960.*
061028	OM. Stores Van. Transferred 3/84. *Formerly LMS PIII BG M31179M, to dia 2007 on lot 1305 Wolverton 1941.*

061029	OM. Stores Van. Transferred 3/84. Formerly LMS PIII BG M31305M, to dia 2007 on lot 1357 Wolverton 1944.
061032	Taunton Engineers' Yard. RCE Tool Van. Transferred 11/83. Previously DW150151. *Formerly Fruit C W2487W.*
061034	BJ. Workshop Van. Transferred 1/84. *Formerly BR Mk1 CCT W94798, to dia 816 on lot 30614 Earlestown 1961.*
061035	BJ. RM & EE Stores Van. Transferred 1/84. *Formerly BR Mk1 CCT W94510, to dia 816 on lot 30563 Earlestown 1960.*
061036	BJ. RM & EE Stores Van. Transferred 1/84. *Formerly BR Mk1 CCT W94555, to dia 816 on lot 30563 Earlestown 1960.*
061046	LA. Stores Van. To be transferred. Previously ADB975784. *Formerly GWR design Siphon G W1006W, to dia O62 on lot 1751 Swindon 1952.*
061047	LA. Stores Van. To be transferred. Previously ADB975785. *Formerly GWR design Siphon G W1310W, to dia O62 on lot 1721 Swindon 1949.*
068725	Radyr Yard. RCE Bridge Department Stores Van. Transferred 10/78. Previously DW150365. *Formerly Fruit D W2807W, to dia Y9 on lot 1606, 1937.*
068746	LA. Stores Van. Transferred 11/78. *Formerly GWR Siphon G W2978W, to dia O33 on lot 1664 Swindon 1945.*
070836	Reading RCE Plant Depot. RCE Stores Van. Transferred 7/79. Previously TDB975172. *Formerly GWR design Fruit D W92048, to dia 805 on lot 30345 Swindon 1958.*
070837	Honeybourne Tip. RCE Staff Van. Transferred 10/79. Previously DW300. *Formerly Goods Brake Van W56322W.*
070840	LE. Sludge Tender. Transferred 9/79. Previously ADW150437. *Formerly R.O.D. Tender.*
070843	Newport Maindee Engineers' Yard. RCE Stores Van. Transferred 7/78. Previously DW150343. *Formerly Fruit C W2815W, to dia Y9 on lot 1606, 1937.*
070844	Newport Maindee Engineers' Yard. RCE Stores Van. Transferred 7/78. Previously DW150357. *Formerly Fruit D W2876W, to dia Y11 on lot 1649, 1939.*
070862	Reading RCE Plant Depot. RCE Stores Van. Transferred 7/79. Previously TDB975174. *Formerly GWR design Fruit D W92053, to dia 805 on lot 30345 Swindon 1958.*
070864	Reading RCE Plant Depot. RCE Stores Van. Transferred 7/79. Previously TDB975173. *Formerly GWR design Fruit D W92049, to dia 805 on lot 30345 Swindon 1958.*
070874	Reading RCE Plant Depot. RCE Stores Van. Transferred 7/79. Previously TDB975299. *Formerly GWR design Fruit D W3404W, to dia Y11 on lot 1723 Swindon 1950.*
070882	Exmouth Jct C&W Shops. Fuel Tank Wagon. Transferred 10/79. *Formerly Milk Tank W2564W, to dia O37, 1932.*

SR — 8xxxx

Allocated numbers have reached 083589 and all vehicles also have their number engraved on a metal plate, the previous identity being obliterated. Most are painted in olive livery and carry a brand indicating the owning department and location of the vehicle. Unless stated otherwise all vehicles are ex-SR.

080336	Southampton Docks. Crane Match Wagon. Transferred 4/54. *Formerly 4 Buf TRB S12518S, to dia 2572 on lot 951 Eastleigh/Lancing 1938.*

082756	RY. Stores Van. Transferred 8/67. *Formerly PMV S1047S.*
082757	Guildford. PSS Staff and Tool Van. Transferred 10/67. Previously DS374. *Formerly SECR PMV S1972S, built 1922.*
082764	ZG. Match Wagon. Transferred 12/67. Previously DS35. *Formerly Ransome and Rapier Breakdown Crane Match Wagon, built 1919.*
082949	ZG. Stores Van. Transferred 1/71. *Formerly CCT S2400S, to dia 361 built Selhurst 1931.*
082962	Basingstoke. Stores Van. Transferred 11/67. *Formerly GUV E96202, converted from an LNER CK on lot 30674 Doncaster 1962.*
083037	Basingstoke, condemned. RM & EE Stores Van. Transferred 7/72. Previously DS3157. *Formerly PMV S1166S, to dia 3103 on RSCO A824 Ashford 1936.*
083055	Fratton Yard. Stores Van. Transferred 11/72. *Formerly PMV S1124S, to dia 3103 on RSCO A855 Ashford 1936.*
083056	Portsmouth and Southsea. Stores Van. Transferred 11/72. *Formerly BR Fish Van E87588, to dia 800 on lot 30344 Faverdale 1960.*
083145	ZG. Test Vehicle. Transferred 5/73. *Formerly 4-Cor TTK S10088S, to dia 2007 on lot 950 Eastleigh/Lancing 1938.*
083146	ZG. Stores Van. Transferred 5/73. *Formerly PMV S1148S, to dia 3103 on RSCO A824 Ashford 1936.*
083185	Horsham, condemned. PSS Staff and Tool Van. Transferrd 3/75. Previously RDS1103. *Formerly PMV S1212S, to dia 3103 on RSCO A824 Ashford 1936.*
083210	Fratton Yard. Generator Van. Transferred 4/75. Previously ADM395941. *Formerly LMS Pl BG M30747M, to dia 1715 on lot 344 Cammell-Laird 1928.*
083211	Fratton Yard. Generator Van. Transferred 4/75. Previously ADM395942. *Formerly LMS Pl BG M30789M, to dia 1715 on lot 344 Cammell-Laird 1928.*
083235	Effingham Junction. Roof Painters Staff and Tool Van. Transferred 6/75. Previously TDB975402. *Formerly B S360S, to dia 3093 on RSCO A927 Ashford/Eastleigh 1938.*
083237	Basingstoke, condemned. RM & EE Stores Van. Transferred 4/76. Previously ADS375. *Formerly SECR PMV S1981S, built 1922.*
083240	Hastings. S&T Stores Van. Transferred 10/76. Previously ADS147. *Formerly PMV S2138S, to dia 3103 on RSCO L1191 Lancing 1942.*
083262	ZG. Equipment Carrier. Transferred 5/78. Previously CDS3151. *Formerly Warwell Wagon No. 34.*
083264	Gl. RM & EE Staff and Stores Coach. Transferred 4/77. *Formerly BR Mk1 TSO S4047, to dia 93 on lot 30149 Ashford/Swindon 1956.*
083268	ZG. Stores Van. Transferred 5/78. *Formerly PMV S1120S, to dia 3013 on RSCO A824 Ashford 1936.*
083285	Strawberry Hill EMU Depot. RM & EE Stores Van. Transferred 7/80. *Formerly PMV S1576S, to dia 3103 on RSCO A3590 Ashford 1950.*
083287	Strawberry Hill EMU Depot. RM & EE Stores Van. Transferred 10/77. Previously KDS152. *Formerly PMV S2200S, to dia 3103 on RSCO A Ashford 1934.*
083318	Fratton Yard. Stores Van. Transferred 3/78. *Formerly LNER CCT E1263E, to dia 6 York 1939.*
083319	Fratton Yard. Stores Van. Transferred 3/78. *Formerly LMS design CCT M37320M, to dia 2026 on lot 1636 Earlestown 1952.*
083320	ZG. Stores Van. Transferred 4/78. *Formerly GWR (Hawksworth) design BG W306W, to dia K45 on lot 1740 Swindon 1950.*
083330	ZG. Stores Van. Transferred 4/78. *Formerly BY S732S, to dia 3092 on RSCO A974 Ashford/Eastleigh 1938.*

083331	ZG. Stores Van. Transferred 4/78. *Formerly GWR (Hawksworth) design BG W311W, to dia K45 on lot 1740 Swindon 1950.*
083336	SE. Stores Van. Transferred 10/80. *Formerly B S379S, to dia 3093 on RSCO A927 Ashford/Eastleigh 1938.*
083346	Basingstoke. Stores Van. Transferred 10/78. *Formerly LMS design CCT M37318M, to dia 2026 on lot 1636 Earlestown 1952.*
083347	Basingstoke. Stores Van. Transferred 10/78. *Formerly LMS design CCT M37227M, to dia 2026 on lot 1770 Swindon 1957.*
083348	Basingstoke. Stores Van. Transferred 10/78. *Formerly LMS design CCT M37217M, to dia 2026 on lot 1770 Swindon 1957.*
083349	Basingstoke. Stores Van. Transferred 10/78. *Formerly LMS design CCT M37223M, to dia 2026 on lot 1770 Swindon 1957.*
083350	Basingstoke, condemned. S&T Staff and Tool Van. Transferred 9/78. Previously KDS102. *Formerly PMV S2183S, to dia 3103 on RSCO A Ashford 1933.*
083351	Basingstoke, condemned. S&T Staff and Tool Van. Transferred 9/78. Previously KDS3062. *Formerly PMV S1223S, to dia 3103 on RSCO A824 Ashford 1936.*
083352	Hither Green PAD. RCE Staff and Tool Van. Transferred 9/78. Previously KDS1102. *Formerly PMV S1190S, to dia 3103 on RSCO A824 Ashford 1936.*
083355	ZG. Stores Van. Transferred 11/78. *Formerly BY S699S, to dia 3092 on RSCO A974 Ashford/Eastleigh 1938.*
083356	ZG. Stores Van. Transferred 11/78. *Formerly BY S412S, to dia 3092 on RSCO A928 Ashford/Eastleigh 1937.*
083357	New Cross Gate PAD. Staff Coach. Transferred 11/78. *Formerly BR Mk1 TTO S3975, to dia 93 on lot 30090 York 1954.*
083361	Salisbury. Stores Van. Transferred 5/79. *Formerly SR design GUV S4588S, to dia 3182 on RSCO A975 Ashford/Eastleigh 1938.*
083372	ZG. Stores Van. Transferred 9/79. *Formerly SR design GUV S4590S, to dia 3182 on RSCO A975 Ashford/Eastleigh 1938.*
083379	ZG. Stores Van. Transferred 10/79. *Formerly SR design GUV S4598S, to dia 3182 on RSCO L3228 Lancing 1949.*
083392	Hoo Junction Tip. RCE Staff and Tool Van. Transferred 3/80. Previously KDS1102. *Formerly PMV S1169S, to dia 3103 on RSCO A824 Ashford 1936.*
083393	Redhill. RCE Staff and Tool Van. Transferred 4/80. Previously ADS70140. *Formerly PMV S2216S, to dia 3103 Ashford 1935.*
083394	Redbridge RCE Works. Stores Van. Transferred 7/80. *Formerly PMV S1628S, to dia 3103 on RSCO A3590 Ashford/Lancing 1950.*
083397	Northam (Down Yard). Stores Van. Transferred 12/80. *Formerly PMV S1613S, to dia 3103 on RSCO A3590 Ashford 1950.*
083402	East Croydon. S&T Stores Van. Transferred 11/80. *Formerly BR Fish Van E87720, to dia 800 on lot 30384 Faverdale 1960.*
083403	Three Bridges S&T Yard. S&T Stores Van. Transferred 11/80. *Formerly BR Fish Van E87820, to dia 800 on lot 30384 Faverdale 1960.*
083409	SL. Instruction Coach for London Fire Brigade. Transferred 2/81. Previously TDS70160. *Formerly Maunsell BTK S3687S, to dia 2105 Eastleigh 1929.*
083410	New Cross Gate C&W Shops. RM & EE Staff and Tool Van. Transferred 11/81. Previously ADS6. *Formerly PMV S1236S, to dia 3103 on RSCO A824 Ashford 1936.*

083428	New Cross Gate C&W Shops. RM & EE Staff and Tool Van. Transferred 11/81. Previously ADS 163. *Formerly PMV S1242S, to dia 3103 on RSCO A825 Ashford 1936.*
083431	Wimbledon Engineers Yard. S&T Stores Van. Transferred 3/82. *Formerly CCT S1987S, to dia 3101 on RSCO A3702 Ashford 1951.*
083432	Wimbledon Engineers Yard. S&T Stores Van. Transferred 3/82. *Formerly CCT S2509S, to dia 3101 on RSCO L3764 Lancing 1955.*
083433	Strawberry Hill EMU Depot. RM & EE Stores Van. Transferred 12/81. *Formerly PMV S1618S, to dia 3103 on RSCO A3590 Ashford 1950.*
083434	CJ. RM & EE Stores Van. Transferred 12/81. *Formerly BR Mk1 CCT S94326 to dia 816 on lot 30562 Earlestown 1960.*
083435	Wimbledon Engineers' Yard. S&T Stores Van. Transferred 3/82. Previously KDS12. *Formerly PMV S2205S, to dia 3103 on RSCO A Ashford 1934.*
083438	Wimbledon Engineers' Yard. RCE Stores Van. Transferred 3/82. *Formerly BR Mk1 CCT S94347, to dia 816 on lot 30562 Earlestown 1960.*
083439	Wimbledon Engineers' Yard. RCE Stores Van. Transferred 3/82. *Formerly BR Mk1 CCT S94752, to dia 816 on lot 30614 Earlestown 1961.*
083469	FR. Stores Van. Transferred 12/82. *Formerly PMV S1854S, to dia 3103 on RSCO L1092 Lancing/Eastleigh 1940.*
083470	FR. Stores Van. Transferred 12/82. *Formerly PMV S2097S, to dia 3103 on RSCO L1191 Lancing 1942.*
083471	FR. Stores Van. Transferred 12/82. *Formerly PMV S1655S, to dia 3103 on RSCO A3590 Ashford/Lancing 1950.*
083475	Eastleigh Dorset Siding. ODM Stores Van. Transferred 6/83. Previously ADS70139. *Formerly PMV S1154S, to dia 3103 on RSCO A824 Ashford 1936.*
083477	Eastleigh Dorset Siding. ODM Staff and Tool Van. Transferred 6/83. *Formerly BY S746S, to dia 3092 on RSCO A974 Ashford/Eastleigh 1938.*
083492	Brighton Engineers' Depot. ODM Stores Coach. Transferred 5/83. *Formerly LSWR Ironclad BTK S3184S, to dia 135 Eastleigh 1921.*
083505	ZG. Stores Van. Transferred 4/84. Previously CDS541. *Formerly Covered Van S49032S, built 1938.*
083506	ZG. Stores Van. Transferred 4/84. Previously CDS1728. *Formerly Covered Van S48913S, built 1937.*
083507	ZG. Stores Van. Transferred 4/84. Previously CDS1817. *Formerly Covered Van S48852S, built 1937.*
083508	ZG. Stores Van. Transferred 4/84. Previously CDS1818. *Formerly Covered Van S49004S, built 1940.*
083521	ZG. Stores Van. Transferred 6/84. Previously ADB977039. *Formerly CCT S1989S, to dia 3101 on RSCO A3702 Ashford 1951.*
083522	ZG. Stores Van. Transferred 6/84. Previously ADB977066. *Formerly B S232S, to dia 3093 on RSCO L1029 Lancing/Eastleigh 1939.*
083523	ZG. Stores Van. Transferred 6/84. Previously ADB975276. *Formerly CCT S1747S, to dia 3101 on RSCO A972 Ashford/Eastleigh 1938.*
083528	ZG. Stores Van. Transferred 4/84. *Formerly PMV S1561S, to dia 3103 on RSCO A3590 Ashford 1950.*
083569	Sandown. RCE Stores Van. Transferred 2/85. *Formerly Isle of Wight S19S, originally LT 3045 built Union Construction Co 1930.*
083571	Waterloo. Stores Van. Transferred 7/84. *Formerly B S205S, to dia 3093 on RSCO L1029 Lancing/Eastleigh 1939.*
083572	Waterloo. Stores Van. Transferred 7/84. *Formerly B S219S, to dia 3093 on RSCO L1029 Lancing/Eastleigh 1939.*
083574	Salisbury. Exhibition Coach. Transferred 12/84. Previously M99607. *Formerly Mk1 BTK W34307, rebuilt as an exhibition coach on lot 30841 Swindon 1972.*

ScR — 09xxxx

Of all the regions the least use of internal users is made by the Scottish Region. The third digit of each 09xxxx range indicates the owning department i.e. 095xxx are RM & EE vehicles, 096xxx are operating department vehicles, 097xxx are RCE vehicles whilst 099xxx are not classified. Highest allocated numbers are 095016, 096054, 097006 and 099001 respectively. The Scottish Region (like the Eastern Region) only paints the new number on, internal user numberplates not being used.

095003	GC. Stores Van. Transferred 11/76. *Formerly LMS PIII BG M30972M, to dia 2007 on lot 1096 Wolverton 1938.*
095014	ML. Stores Van. Transferred 2/82. *Formerly LMS PIII BG M31190M, to dia 2007 on lot 1305 Wolverton 1941.*
095016	ML. Stores Van. Transferrd 10/84. *Formerly LMS PIII BG M31122M, to dia 2007 on lot 1304 Derby 1941.*
096011	Perth Freight Depot. Stores Van. Transferred 10/76. Previously TDM396004. *Formerly LMS GUV M37715M, to dia 1870 on lot 750 Wolverton 1934.*
096012	Perth Freight Depot. Stores Van. Transferred 10/76. Previously TDM396002. *Formerly LMS CCT M37124M, to dia 2026 on lot 1154 Metro-Cammell 1938.*
096039	Thurso. Stores Van. Transferred 5/78. *Formerly GWR BG W130W, to dia on lot 1652 Swindon 1940.*
096040	Glasgow Shieldhall. Cartic Ramp. Transferred 5/78. Previously TDB975093. *Formerly BR Mk1 TK SC24728, to dia 146 on lot 30073 Wolverton 1953.*
097004	Perth Engineers' Yard. RCE Staff and Dormitory Coach. Transferred 12/83. Previously DE321053 and 'NE Div 6'. *Formerly LNER CK SC18241E, to dia 296 Doncaster 1939 (originally 32431).*
099000	IS. Stores Van. Transferred 10/80. *Formerly LMS PIII BG M31265M, to dia 2007 on lot 1357 Wolverton 1944.*

024497, an ex BR standard CCT is seen in the Yard of BREL Litchurch Lane Works on 16th September 1984. [C. J. Tuffs